FAUST AS MUSICIAN

FAUST
AS MUSICIAN

A Study of Thomas Mann's novel
Doctor Faustus

by

PATRICK CARNEGY

1973

CHATTO & WINDUS
LONDON

Published by
Chatto & Windus Ltd
42 William IV Street
London W.C.2.

*

Clarke, Irwin & Co. Ltd
Toronto

ISBN 0 7011 1928 4

© Patrick Carnegy 1973

Printed in Great Britain by
Butler & Tanner Ltd
Frome and London

ACKNOWLEDGEMENTS

Many people have helped me in the preparation of this book and I am deeply grateful to them all. I should particularly like to thank D. J. Enright, Jim Ford, Jon Harris, Erich Heller, Peter Heyworth, Paul Roubiczek, Eric Sams, Ulrich Simon and John M. Thomson for their encouragement and constructive suggestions.

It is a pleasure to thank Frau Katja Mann and the Estate of Arnold Schoenberg for permission to reprint the letters by Thomas Mann and Arnold Schoenberg which first appeared in *The Saturday Review of Literature*. I am also glad to thank Secker and Warburg Ltd. and Alfred A. Knopf Inc. for permission to quote from, and occasionally to revise, Mrs H. T. Lowe-Porter's translations of Mann's works.

Contents

'. . . music was only foreground and representation, only a paradigm for something more general, only a means to express the situation of art in general, of culture, even of man and the intellect itself in our so critical era. A novel of music? Yes. But it was also conceived as a novel of the culture and the era.'

THE GENESIS OF A NOVEL, p. 37.

CHAPTER ONE

Introduction

Thomas Mann's novel *Doctor Faustus* is the imaginary biography of the German composer Adrian Leverkühn as told by his friend Serenus Zeitblom. Written between 1943 and 1947 while Mann was living in exile in America, it is the culmination of a lifetime's study of German musicality. Mann had long believed that music brought out the best and the worst in the German spirit. However, as he himself said, *Doctor Faustus* is not merely a novel of music, because music stands as paradigm and metaphor in what might more rightly be described as 'a novel of the culture and the era' (GN, 37).* His just and formidable analysis of a musical culture in decline is also a pathology of modern civilization: the twofold indictments of 'bloody barbarism' and of 'bloodless intellectualism' levelled by Zeitblom at Leverkühn's penultimate composition, the *Apocalypsis cum Figuris*, stand for Mann's own criticism of the Germany of the Third Reich.

In *Doctor Faustus* Mann takes up the principal themes of his earlier writings, especially those of disease and cultural dissolution, bringing them together into a more comprehensive and personal treatment than he had ever attempted before. The novel bears a heavy confessional burden: it is a retrospective assessment of his artistic achievement and the price he had to pay for it. It is a

* See Bibliography, p. 174, for key to abbreviated titles, and for details of publications cited by title alone.

long, difficult book which presupposes familiarity with the
German mind and its culture. It draws on texts familiar
and unfamiliar, classic and contemporary, and has no
special respect for other people's intellectual 'property' – a
fact to which the composer Arnold Schoenberg (whose
12-tone Method was transplanted unacknowledged into
the book) was to take some exception. It is an elaborate
montage whose materials are drawn not only from literature and philosophy, but also from science, theology,
musicology, and of course from the Faust legend itself.

Mann's novel has some claim to be considered as the
definitive Faust story of our time. This new Faust is not
seeking Enlightenment, as was Goethe's, but artistic
inspiration: he is a musician because music is supreme
among the arts. He sins in striking a pact with the devil,
consciously contracting a syphilitic infection to revitalize
an imagination stifled by excess of Enlightenment. He
deploys magic and the irrational against reason and
intellect, as had done the Faust of the sixteenth-century
chapbook, whom he follows to certain damnation. The
resonance of this early Faust story echoes throughout
Mann's version, whole sections of it being worked, almost
verbatim, into his own text.

In *The Magic Mountain* disease was the necessary condition for the education of Hans Castorp, the bourgeois
dreamer and would-be engineer. In *Doctor Faustus*,
disease has become the necessary condition for art. In
Mann's own words, 'it is a means provided by the devil
to induce creativity in an artist inhibited by knowledge'.*
The artist sins in seeking out that disease, but his sin is
treated by Mann as the higher morality of the artist, a
morality of creative disobedience with which Mann is
much concerned. He shows the disastrous consequences

* *Letters of Thomas Mann*, p. 599.

when this privileged morality (for which the artist himself often pays a terrible toll) is assumed by the masses as
their own. Mann suggests more powerfully in *Doctor
Faustus* than in his other writings that the rise of National
Socialism in a wilderness of indifference and political im-
maturity was nothing other than a monstrous flowering
of the German soul. How far, Mann asks, does the artist's
proper self-absorption in his work exempt him from
personal, social and political responsibility? Can art be
a justifiable activity when there would seem to be so many
more urgent claims upon energy and effort? Indeed, has
artistic activity any longer the slightest validity? 'There's
no question about it,'Mann wrote to Bruno Walter in 1945
when asking for technical criticism and advice, 'music as
well as all the other arts–and not only the arts–is in a
crisis which sometimes seems to threaten its very life.'* In
Doctor Faustus these agonized doubts are worked out in
the lonely preoccupations of a creative mind, committed
to nothing less than the total renewal of a declining art.

In Leverkühn Mann makes the experiment of assuming an inspirational breakthrough due to a pact with the
devil. Just how successful Mann intended this breakthrough to be, how good Leverkühn's music was meant
to be, and whether Leverkühn *had* opened up the path
to a new and blither music of the future, are problematic
issues, as we shall see later. We do know that Mann profoundly hoped that there would be a future for art. His
idea was that after its disintegration in complexity, art
might attain a new-found serenity and directness, even
as he hoped that the best of the German spirit might
revive and flourish again after the war. 'A *way out*
must be found,' he wrote to a correspondent in 1944,
'many modern artists feel that way . . . Agreed, the way

* *Letters of Thomas Mann*, p. 465.

will hardly go back beyond what was preparing in *Tristan* and *Parsifal* and then took its course.'*

For Mann these were personal as well as general questions. Later in this essay we shall try to assess how well he was able to answer them by his juxtaposition of the hermetic life of his Faustian hero with a bitter commentary on the rise and fall of Nazi Germany.

Our present purpose is to consider the leading ideas of a great novel, to relate them to their background, and to pursue some of their implications. In German the literature on Mann is vast enough, but there is comparatively little of significance in English, either on Mann's work as a whole (with the outstanding exception of Erich Heller's *Thomas Mann The Ironic German*), or on individual novels. At least three of these, namely *The Magic Mountain*, *Joseph and his Brothers* and *Doctor Faustus* are of sufficient stature and complexity to be no less deserving of detailed discussion than such favourite subjects as *Ulysses*, *Finnegans Wake* and *À la Recherche du Temps Perdu*. Hermann Weigand's pioneering book *Thomas Mann's Novel, Der Zauberberg* (New York, 1933) is still very well worth reading but of *Doctor Faustus* only two studies are available in English, both translations from the German. The first is Mann's own description of how he conceived and worked on *Doctor Faustus, The Genesis of a Novel*;† the second is *Doctor Faustus: the Sources and Structure of the Novel* by Dr Gunilla Bergsten, a dissertation published in 1963 in America. This well-researched study offers valuable insights into the novel, and contains an excellent bibliography. But these two books leave many questions open.

In the following pages no attempt will be made to

* *Letters of Thomas Mann*, p. 452.
† *The Story of a Novel* (Knopf).

present a thesis, or a conventional exercise in analytical literary criticism. No evaluation will be offered of the novel's 'standing', nor of its structure, characterization, plot and use of dialogue. The primary concern will be Mann's intellectual ideas and their sources. This essay examines some of the more perplexing inconsistencies and difficulties without attempting to resolve such fundamentally unresolvable conflicts as that between the artist's autonomous aesthetic philosophy and his ethical responsibilities as citizen. Much of the criticism and comparative study is speculative in nature and leads to no tidy conclusions.

The first three chapters establish the novel's principal poles, its musical and its political aspects, whose relationship will be taken up more fully later. We shall first try to say something of the significance of music in Mann's life and to see why he chose to make his Faust a musician.

*   *   *

Mann went to great trouble to ensure that the musical details in *Doctor Faustus* should be authentic. His principal musical collaborator was the critic, philosopher and sociologist, T. W. Adorno, but Mann also received technical assistance from his own son Michael, from Bruno Walter, from Arnold Schoenberg and from many others. It was, Mann said, 'of supreme importance to achieve precise realization of the means and the foreground' (GN, 37). After literature it was music which lay closest to Mann's sensibility. As a boy he had played the violin, and thereafter he was a diligent student of musical theory (GBF, 73). It must have seemed to him that many of his personal artistic problems and those of his time could suggestively be approached by projecting them in extreme form into the musical world. From Hanno Buddenbrook onwards, music and musicians had always

featured prominently in his short stories and novels;
there had been the notable essays on Wagner, and now
there was Faustus-Leverkühn. Mann recalled that his
earliest note about a Faust story went back to 1901, and
he drew attention to 'how long this project had had to
stand in line waiting its turn, waiting for the "fullness
of time" ' (GN, 53). By 1945, in the middle of work on
the novel, he was sure that it had been

> a grave error on the part of legend and story not to con-
> nect Faust with music. . . . Music is both calculated order
> and chaos-breeding irrationality. It is rich in conjuring
> incantatory gestures, in magic of numbers, the most un-
> realistic and yet the most impassioned of arts, mystical and
> abstract. If Faust is to be the representative of the German
> soul, he would have to be musical, for the relation of the
> German to the world is abstract and mystical, that is,
> musical . . . *

Mann's musical sympathies were, though, as we shall
see, very much at variance with his twentieth-century
material. 'I understand the New Music only very
theoretically,' he wrote, 'though I know something of it,
I cannot really enjoy and love it. I have after all publicly
explained that the triad-world of the *Ring* is basically my
musical home.'† Mann considered music after Wagner
as an art in decline. While writing the last pages of
Faustus he 'once again heard Schubert's glorious B flat
major Trio, and meditated while I listened on the happy
state of music that it represented, on the destiny of the
musical art since then – a lost paradise' (GN, 181). As for
his taste for the music of his own time, not even the

* From 'Germany and the Germans', an address delivered on May
29th, 1945, in the Library of Congress, published in *Thomas Mann's
Addresses*.
† Letter of October 19th, 1951, to H. H. Stuckenschmidt in the
latter's *Arnold Schoenberg*.

advocacy of his eminent composer friends assisted him to more than a 'very theoretical' understanding. The very act of writing *Faustus* is critical, and self-critical, of times in which the 'new music' often flourishes more vigorously in the words and explanations to which it gives rise than in the actual notes themselves.

Mann reasoned that somewhere along the line something had gone seriously wrong, 'and now the question is whether at the present stage of our consciousness, our knowledge, our sense of truth, this little game is still permissible, still intellectually possible' (180). Perhaps social reasons were partly to blame: 'Complete insecurity, problematic conditions, and lack of harmony of our social situation.' Music had acquired a conscience about these things.

But even if music was a lost paradise and he could not bring himself to believe in the Schoenbergian renewal, Mann bent himself to study the new music and what had gone wrong with it. We are told that Leverkühn, in his early compositions, was giving of his best to things in which he no longer believed. In *Doctor Faustus*, a seasoned late work, Mann found himself doing something very similar in having to provide weighty discussions of a music in which he never had believed. One wonders how much attention he paid to music written outside the charmed Schoenberg circle into which he—like so many others—was so powerfully drawn. Just as his susceptibility to earlier music had been ruled by Wagner, so now his scepticism about modern music was ruled by Schoenberg.

The ease with which the Nazis appropriated Mann's 'musical home' for their particular purposes—Hitler at Bayreuth—shook his faith to its foundations. In time he came to see this as the most painful proof of all that music,

B

like Wagner's Kundry, serves not only the powers of
light but those of darkness as well.

*   *   *

Mann was once asked whether he had had any model
in mind for Leverkühn. No, he replied, Leverkühn was
an invented character, yet one whom he hoped would
be able to take his place 'among the real situations and
personalities of modern musical life'. But at other times
Mann freely acknowledged that Leverkühn (the name
being a pointed composite of 'leben' = to live, and 'kühn'
= bold) was modelled on real life figures, in particular
on Nietzsche. Nietzsche's influence is immediately recognizable in that Leverkühn's genius is also bound up with
a reclusive life, acute physical suffering and eventual insanity. The extent of the debt to the model is well illustrated by Leverkühn's letter to Zeitblom in which he
describes his first escape from the infected prostitute
Esmeralda. This is virtually identical with Nietzsche's
letter to Paul Deussen about a visit to a Cologne brothel.
Several passages in the novel are taken more or less verbatim from the many Nietzsche books in Mann's working
library–which included several editions of his works and
some twenty-five books about him (GBF, 59).

Other of Leverkühn's characteristics are taken from
the lives of Schumann, Wolf, Tchaikovsky, Mahler,
Dostoevsky and many others. Tchaikovsky's Frau von
Meck, for instance, corresponds to the Mme. de Tolna
who sends Leverkühn the ring with the motto, 'Flee
profane ones! Depart'! (393). The death of Mahler's
child Maria parallels that of Leverkühn's sole consolation, the angelic little boy Echo.

Dostoevsky's ideas abound–Leverkühn's encounter
with the devil, for example, is modelled on much the

same lines as that of Ivan Karamazov; Mann wrote that 'under the sign of *Faustus*, I was greatly drawn to Dostoevsky's grotesque, apocalyptic realm of suffering, in contrast with my usual preference for Tolstoy's Homeric, primal strength' (GN, 102). While Leverkühn is writing the final masterpiece which immediately precedes his madness, his creator, so he tells us, was re-reading *The House of the Dead*. But the most controversial source for Leverkühn was Mann's contemporary and, until the publication of *Doctor Faustus*, his friend, the composer Arnold Schoenberg, to whom we shall have cause to return later.

Mann has been criticized* for making such extensive use of nineteenth-century material for a book which is so largely about our own century. There are three points to be set against this objection. First, that the technical music practice attributed to Leverkühn is, after all, of the twentieth century, being based directly on Schoenberg's 12-tone Method; second, that if one should consider, as Mann certainly did, that the nineteenth century was where most of the trouble sprang from in the first place, then one is bound to trace it back to its source; and thirdly, the novel's marked autobiographical aspect—for Mann intended it also as a record of his own intellectual development which, he freely admitted, was dominated by the nineteenth century.

It is certainly a beguiling idea to present a fictional fulfilment of the Nietzschean prophesies which had turned the mind that had dared to pronounce them. For in *Doctor Faustus*, extreme implications of Nietzsche's ideas are put on trial. The consequences are such that at

* See for example, a review of *Die Entstehung des Doktor Faustus*, the original German edition of *The Genesis of a Novel*, in *The Times Literary Supplement*, August 26th, 1949.

times one suspects that the author's intention is to suggest
that man's proper response to his condition begins with
the rejection of hope and matures in the acceptance of
despair. But this is not so, for ultimately Mann departs
from Nietzsche and affirms his belief that, out of the
irremediable, hope might one day germinate. In Mann's
words, 'It would be but a hope beyond hopelessness, the
transcendence of despair—not betrayal to her, but the
miracle that passes belief.' This idea is by no means new
to his thought; 'At the very moment of uttermost terror',
he wrote in *Fiorenza* (1904) of Brother Girolamo's ser-
mon, 'a miracle comes to pass. The annihilating wrath
upon his countenance melts away. . . . "The miracle of
grace!" he cries. "It comes to pass!" ' (SOL1, 251).

Mann's intentions in *Faustus* are made plain by his
first thoughts on the outcome of Leverkühn's life's work.
In *Genesis* he describes how in his first draft of the description of Leverkühn's last composition he 'had been too
optimistic, too kindly, . . . had been too lavish with the
consolation' (GN, 176). After Adorno had criticized the
passage he sat down next morning to a thorough over-
hauling of the one and a half or two pages concerned
'and gave them the circumspect form they now have'.

It is the final positive note, however faintly sounded,
which lifts the book above a mere pathological study. It
inevitably affects our view of Leverkühn's musical development in search of a renaisssance of the art. However
tentatively the 'voice of mourning' may have eventually
given way before the 'light in the night', the hope of
renewal that threads the book is to be read as sincere
rather than ironic in intent. It is unlikely that Mann
would have been able to identify himself as closely as he
confessed to have done with a Leverkühn whose artistic
output he considered to be totally sterile.

While engaged upon *Faustus* Mann consulted many eminent musicians. His diary records dining with the Schoenbergs and an evening at the Franz Werfels' when he sounded out Stravinsky's views on Schoenberg. Stravinsky's own recollection of this evening is worth quotation:

> Mann liked musical discussions, and his own favourite theme was that music is the art most remote from life, the art that needs no *experience*. Mann was a professorial figure, with an erect, almost stiff-necked posture, characteristically, and with his left hand often in its coat pocket. . . . Mann was virtuous—i.e., courageous, patient, kind, sincere; I think he may have been a profound pessimist, too. *

On another occasion Mann wrote in his diary, 'Buffet dinner at Schoenbergs' to celebrate his [Schoenberg's] sixty-ninth birthday. Many guests. Talked with Gustav Arlt, Klemperer, Frau Heims-Reinhardt. Spent some time with Klemperer and Schoenberg. Talked too much . . .' (GN, 45). However much he may have talked and however much they may have talked modern music to him, there is little evidence that he actually heard a great deal. He reports that he listened to music at this time with 'extreme and objective attentiveness' but there follows no list of Schoenberg, Webern, Hindemith, Stravinsky or other moderns, only Haydn, Mozart, Beethoven *et al.* One exception was Berg. In October 1948 (after the book's completion, but surely a representative sample of his musical interest) he listed his current favourite records:

> Franck: D minor Symphony. Mendelssohn: Concerto in E minor for Violin. 'Mozart and Others'—a song recital by

* Igor Stravinsky and Robert Craft, *Expositions and Developments*, Faber and Faber, London, 1962, p. 78.

Lotte Lehmann. Berlioz: *Harold in Italy*. Beethoven: '*Eroica*'. Wagner: *Parsifal* Act III, *Walküre* Act I. Berg: *Wozzeck*. Strauss (Johann): Overtures and Waltzes. Schubert: 'Der Musensohn' and 'Der Wanderer', sung by Gerhard Hüsch. Schumann: 'Romanze' (Geibel) and Schubert: 'Der Erlkonig', sung by Heinrich Schlusnus.

The list was completed by

Roosevelt — 'A prayer for the Nation on D-Day. June 6, 1944.' *

Wozzeck excepted, even in those days this is hardly the record collection of a student of twentieth-century music. Nevertheless while his diary carries the confession that 'technical music studies frighten and bore me', Mann conscientiously set himself to deepen his theoretical knowledge. He penetrated 'by reading and research, into the realm of musical technique, life and creativity, just as I had, in the interest of the *Joseph* novels, for example, penetrated into the world of Orientalism, primitive religion, and myth' (GN, 36). There were frequent gatherings at the Werfels' with the Schoenbergs present. 'Pumped S. a great deal on music and the life of a composer' (GN, 27), his diary records and we know that Schoenberg lent Mann a copy of his *Harmonielehre* and gave him a *Jakobsleiter* text.† Schoenberg and Hanns Eisler were even persuaded to go through the harmonic system of *Parsifal* at the piano, to search for unresolved dissonances. They found one–in the Amfortas part of the last act. Afterwards, the two musicians 'explained archaic forms of variation . . . and Schoenberg presented me

---

* List contributed by Mann to *The Saturday Review of Literature*, October 30th, 1948, but not here quoted verbatim.

† Article by Schoenberg in *Music Survey*, 1949, Vol. II, No. 2.

with a pencilled sheet of notes and figures to illustrate them' (GN, 86).

And so the accumulation of material went on, with Mann eagerly picking the mind of any musician who came his way. Some of the book's misrepresentations of modern music must be attributable to unintentional distortions in his recording of these conversations. Others, as we shall see, were made deliberately to suit his case.

Mann soon realized that however valuable conversational advice and reading might be, his subject cried out for a technical collaborator. In the summer of 1943 when engaged on the seventh chapter of *Faustus*, in which are described the attractions held for the young Leverkühn by his uncle's store of musical instruments, Mann came upon the writings of T. W. Adorno whose musical philosophizings, he discovered, had 'the strangest affinity to the idea of my book' (GN, 38). With a pen dipped in the ink of Nietzsche and Karl Kraus, Adorno had written of 'the dire consequences that must flow from the constructivist Schoenbergian approach to music' (GN, 40). The subjection of music to rigorous rational analysis, suggested Adorno, led to the converse of rationality and a casting back of the art into a dark, mythological realm. What was more, Adorno, who had studied with Alban Berg, lent formidable technical support to his speculations. An American singer who had worked with him once remarked to Mann, 'It is incredible. He knows every note in the world' (GN, 39). Adorno deserves no small praise for his intellectual courage—of the Schoenberg circle he was almost alone in daring to mingle criticism with the reverence expected by the composer. As Schoenberg was always on the defensive, this meant that there had ceased to be any significant intercourse between the Master and himself.

Adorno was quickly put to work. In the last pages of chapter seven, the fifteen-year-old Leverkühn is discovered by Zeitblom at the harmonium in his uncle's music shop experimenting with chords of ambiguous tonality, and practising modulations. 'In principle', wrote Mann with Adorno at his elbow, 'he [Leverkühn] showed himself aware of enharmonic changes and not unaware of certain tricks by which one can by-pass keys and use the enharmonic change for modulations' (47). When it is shortly arranged that Leverkühn is to have twice weekly lessons from Wendell Kretschmar, the organist of Kaisersaschern Cathedral,* we can be sure who was really receiving those lessons and from whom. That splendid stuttering enthusiast Kretschmar can hardly have owed much to Adorno, but what he had to say clearly did. Adorno's explanations and private performances for Mann of Beethoven's last piano sonata gave birth to Kretschmar's lecture: 'Why Beethoven failed to write a third movement for the Piano Sonata Opus 111.' 'It is without doubt a matter worth discussing', Zeitblom tells us, 'But think of it in the light of the posters outside the hall of Activities for the Common Weal, or inserted in the Kaisersaschern *Railway Journal*, and ask yourself the amount of public interest it could arouse. People positively did not want to know why Op.111 has only two movements. We who were present at the explanation had indeed an uncommonly enriching evening . . .' (51). In gratitude, Mann slipped Adorno's patronymic Wiesengrund (meadowland) into his description of the Arietta theme (54).

Adorno and Mann had each worked their way to a

* The name itself may have been suggested by that of the music historian Hermann Kretschmar (1848–1924) (GBF, 27). In Mann's original German the name is spelt 'Kretzschmar', thus evoking a Nietzschean association.

cultural philosophy close to the other's. What they
thought they had discovered was a cultural crisis of unprecedented seriousness, a closeness to sterility and the
onset of 'the innate despair that prepares the ground for a
pact with the devil' (GN, 54). Adorno provided faggots
for laying round the feet of the heretic in order to purge
him, so that the soul might live. Mann clearly felt
that Adorno himself shared something of Leverkühn's temperament, as may be gathered from his
reference to 'the tragically cerebral relentlessness of his
[Adorno's] criticism of the contemporary musical situation' (GN, 54). This comment rebounds upon its author
who had also come to believe that the situation had become 'too critical to be dealt with without critique' (240),
even if he had to leave it to Leverkühn's devil to say so
for him.

Never, wrote Mann, had he loved a creature of his
imagination more than Leverkühn–neither Thomas
Buddenbrook, nor Hans Castorp, nor Aschenbach, nor
Joseph, nor the Goethe of *Lotte in Weimar*. The only
possible exception he could find to make was that of
Hanno Buddenbrook. In *Genesis* he records how deeply
the writing of *Faustus* moved him–and more so than
with any previous book. It was 'confession and sacrifice
through and through and hence would not be bound by
considerations of mere discretion' (GN, 73). This leads us
to Mann's close identification with his two main characters, as does also his refusal to describe Leverkühn's physical appearance (something that *The Saturday Review* lost
no time in putting right when it noticed the book). 'Only
the characters more remote from the centre of the book
could be novelistic figures in the picturesque sense . . .
not the two protagonists, who had too much to conceal,
namely the secret of their being identical with each other'

(GN, 75). To depict Leverkühn's outer appearance, he
said, was instantly to threaten him with spiritual down-
fall, 'to diminish and render banal his representativeness'.
But the impossibility of so doing went further than that.
'How mysteriously forbidden it was, how impossible, in a
way I had never felt before!' The truth was that Mann
had projected much of himself into Leverkühn and his
'biographer'. Writing to Paul Amann on October 21st,
1948, he described Zeitblom as 'a parody of myself', and
indeed on the very first page of the novel Zeitblom en-
gagingly describes himself as 'addressed to reason and
harmony . . . not lacking all contact with the arts (I play
the viola d'amore) . . .'. Turning to Leverkühn, Mann
told his friend that 'In Adrian's attitude toward life there
is more of my own than one might think—or than the
reader is intended to think.'* Zeitblom is that part of him
which felt that the world had been turned upside down,
yet found it difficult to live as though this were the case
or even to recognize the possible implications. Thus, at
the very beginning of the novel, in the first of the many
apologies with which the narrator attempts to wash his
hands of the devilish business, he feels it his remaining
inescapable duty to relate, he describes how he

> unhesitatingly resigned my beloved teaching profession,
> and that before the time when it became evident that it
> could not be reconciled with the spirit and claims of our
> historical development. In this respect I am content with
> myself. But my self-satisfaction or, if you prefer, my
> ethical narrow-mindedness can only strengthen my doubt
> whether I may feel myself truly called to my present
> task. (4)

Mann naturally makes sure that Zeitblom's stance is
sufficiently ironic to allow him to slide out of any direct

* *Letters to Paul Amann*, p. 115.

autobiographical confrontation—it is characteristic that Mann should place his narrator inside Germany while he himself was in America at Zeitblom's time of writing. But Zeitblom is a doubly ironic figure; in the bourgeois commentator may be seen the very values which are the targets for Mann's irony. George Steiner has well argued *Faustus* to be a turning point 'because it shows how the classic form and claims of the novel are inseparable from the bias of a middleclass, humanistic culture, how their ruin is a common one'.*

It seems likely that Mann concentrated his habitual all-embracing irony in his narrator so that he might present the principal character in a more direct, confessional way than might otherwise have been possible. Thus Leverkühn's story is told with comparative directness, although the reader has only to remember that it is in fact *Zeitblom*'s story to assume the more comfortable ironic perspective. Mann projects into Leverkühn the tension in his mind between the apprehension of overwhelming difficulties (political, artistic and personal) and the feeling that if solutions were to be found then they would inevitably be extremely painful. Not surprisingly perhaps, this feeling is typical of the masochistic desires of the 'profound pessimist' that Stravinsky saw in Thomas Mann.

In Mann's novel these 'desires' are projected into a fictional character with whom the author closely identified himself. Perhaps there was far more of Mann in Leverkühn than even he acknowledged; beneath the story of the composer's life runs the powerful undertow of the writer's hopes and fears. In the high moral tone of his treatment of the political and artistic themes, Mann makes no attempt to smooth over the occasional doubt

* *Language and Silence*, Faber and Faber, London, 1967, p. 102.

that he had failed to translate *his* own values into effective social attitudes as successfully as he might. No wonder the writing of *Doctor Faustus* cost him so much pain, for this failure in himself was that very failure which the book lays so accusingly at the doors of German artists and intellectuals.

CHAPTER TWO

The Supremacy of Music

Mann often drew attention to 'inwardness' as perhaps the most characteristic German quality, and to German music as its best expression. Thus it comes as no mystery that Mann should think of his Faust, of his Germany, as a musician. The influence of Schopenhauer, Wagner and Nietzsche is at its most evident here, for Mann, like them, seems to have subscribed to the view that music is the supreme mode of artistic expression; and not merely that, but also that it is a form of knowledge too profound for revelation through mere words, and is the highest metaphysical activity. Of other extra-verbal languages, such as the mathematical and the visual, Mann, the philological student, seems to have known too little to have been able to take them into his assessment. In music he recognized the direct language of the will, as Schopenhauer had so described it, the language of the unconscious, of the irrational, which although set down with certitude, yet was ultimately untranslatable and unknowable; a seductive admixture of the rational and the irrational at their most intense.

There is even more to it than that. For just as Mann considered music apt for symbolical treatment of political, social, philosophical and religious problems, so also his own problems as a writer, a man of words, could be projected into the world of music. Like Nietzsche before him, Mann was deeply envious of the musician. In *The Birth*

of Tragedy (*out of the Spirit of Music*, as the title originally ran), Nietzsche describes himself as

> stammering out laborious, arbitrary phrases in an alien
> tongue—as though the speaker were not quite sure him-
> self whether he preferred speech to silence. And, indeed,
> this 'new soul' should have *sung*, not spoken. What a pity
> that I could not tell as a poet what demanded to be told! *

In 1868 Nietzsche confided to a friend that he was looking
for 'some philological matter that could be treated music-
ally' and that on finding it he would 'stammer like a
baby and pile up images, like a barbarian lost in dreams
in the presence of an antique Venus-head'.† Nietzsche
actually did compose music, although his efforts in this
field were indeed infantile, Wagner and Hans von Bülow
being embarrassed and irritated when the philosopher
sought their opinions on his compositions.‡ Mann, for all
his devotion to music, never tempted an alien muse to
make a fool of him, though we may fairly speculate that
Mann the writer, thinker, and teller of tales, must
occasionally have felt less than total confidence in his own
craft of mere words which, as it had for Nietzsche, must
often have seemed inadequate to what he would have liked
to be able to utter. Wagner and Nietzsche had settled for

---

* *The Birth of Tragedy*, translated by W. A. Haussmann, London,
1923, p. 6 (translation revised).

† Quoted in Elliott Zuckerman, *The First Hundred Years of
Wagner's Tristan*, New York, 1964, p. 65.

‡ Hearing of von Bülow's enthusiasm about *The Birth of Tragedy*,
Nietzsche sent him a manuscript piano piece in the hope that he
would perform it at one of his concerts. Von Bülow bluntly replied:
'Your *Manfred Meditation* is the most fantastically extravagant, the
most unedifying, the most anti-musical thing I have come across for
a long time in the way of notes put on paper. Several times I had to
ask myself whether it is all a joke, whether, perhaps, your object was
to produce a parody of the so-called music of the future.' (Quoted in
Ernest Newman, *The Life of Richard Wagner*, Volume 4, New
York, 1946, p. 324.)

the theoretical idea that 'the "Apollonian" drama functions
as intermediary between the audience and the otherwise
incomprehensible or unbearable "Dionysian" music'. As
a writer, Mann knew that it was *his* practical business to
channel Dionysian intuitions into Apollonian prose.
Doubtless the example of Goethe, another of his mentors,
was of service to him here.

   Although Mann's own musical aspirations stopped short
of practice—his lifelong preoccupation with words left
little enough time for that—his writing does show 'musical' tendencies. Most notable is his creative homage to
Wagner, paid by certain applications of what he understood to be Wagner's musical techniques, principally of
the leitmotif, to literary construction—although this is
never taken as far, or employed as thoroughly, as in
Wagner's music. This literary leitmotif technique is as
evident in Mann's significantly named early story *Tristan*
as it is in *Doctor Faustus*. On reading the first three
chapters of the novel to Franz Werfel, Mann was de-
lighted that he

> picked out one of the small motifs of the book, the kind I
> most enjoy working with—like, say, the erotic motif of the
> blue and black eyes; the mother motif; the parallelism of
> the landscapes; or, more significant and essential, ranging
> through the whole book and appearing in many variations,
> the motif of cold, which is related to the motif of laughter.
> (GN, 60)

   The use of motifs and leitmotifs in literature certainly
need not evoke musical comparisons, yet Mann leaves his
reader in no doubt as to his intention to give *Doctor
Faustus* a 'musical' construction. In *Genesis of a Novel* he
described how musical form had long been his ideal.
Referring to his plans for *Doctor Faustus*, he said that
musical form was something 'for which this time there

was a special aesthetic necessity. I felt clearly that my
book itself would have to become the thing it dealt with:
namely, constructivist music' (GN, 54–5). This is a somewhat peculiar notion, but it is best understood as referring
not only to the structural web spun by the recurrent
literary leitmotifs in *Doctor Faustus*, but also to the fact
that the novel incorporates material from a large number
of 'ready made' sources. To a very considerable extent the
novel is a montage, constructed from thinly disguised
borrowings from such diverse sources as the old Faust
chapbook of 1587, scientific material from books and
newspaper cuttings, Nietzsche biography, and twentieth-
century musical theory, to mention only some of the
most readily recognizable material.*

Mann also uses 'music' in *Faustus* as a paradigm for
language. He felt that many problems of verbal language
appeared in extreme and generalized character in music.
To understand why he believed that this was so, we must
pause to consider how music came to occupy its pre-
eminent place in late-Romantic thought.

*   *   *

Beethoven said of his symphonies that in them

> one can feel that something eternal, infinite, never wholly
> comprehensible, is contained in every product of the
> human spirit . . . (Speak to Goethe about this, tell him to
> listen to my symphonies, for then he will admit that music
> is the only entrance to the higher world of knowledge
> which, although it embraces me, a man cannot grasp.)†

* Gunilla Bergsten devotes a lengthy chapter (GBF, 10–98) to the
source material for *Doctor Faustus*. Much of this material was drawn
not only from written sources, but also from Mann's friends and
acquaintances.

† From a conversation with Bettina Brentano, translated by
Michael Hamburger in *Beethoven: Letters, Journals and Conversations*, Jonathan Cape, London, 1951.

Although Goethe might not have agreed, many of those who followed him were only too ready to do so. Chief among them was the influential Schopenhauer, in whose thought music achieves its highest exaltation. For him, music is the purest representation of the theoretical 'secret history of our will'. It is not concerned in any way with copying or representing the Platonic 'Ideas' (as architecture and other plastic and literary arts are) but is only about itself. Form and content are inseparable. Thus the composer reveals 'the innermost nature of the world and expresses the profoundest wisdom in a language which his reason does not understand'.* Music performs unconsciously what philosophy tries to do consciously. This preference for the irrational naturally has a dangerous side, for it is here that we are most susceptible, whether to the true or the false, as Mann was only too well aware.

Schopenhauer became the favourite philosopher of the composer of *Tristan und Isolde* where the Word is arguably more completely swallowed by the Tone than in any of Wagner's other operas, although in this and other works by the author of the theory of the *Gesamtkunstwerk*, a certain confusion between the proper functions of Word and Tone is only too apparent. Thanks to the enormous influence of Wagner's art, Schopenhauer's doctrine became the creed of a generation of writers and poets, no less than of composers themselves.

Of the ways in which the literary and visual arts aspired towards the 'condition of music' we are here not concerned in detail. It is enough to notice the long-lasting and probably indelible effect of music on the literary arts, and in particular on the work of even so thoroughgoingly

* Schopenhauer, *The World as Will and Representation*, translated by E. F. J. Payne, New York, 1966, Vol. 1, p. 260.

c

literary an artist as Mann. After Beethoven and Wagner,
Mann recognized, the relation between literature and
music needed redefining:

> Wagner's music is not really 'music' any more than his
> dramatic structure (which it fleshes out to make an opera,
> a living work of art) is literature. . . . The texts round
> which it twines, filling out their dramatic content, are not
> literature—but the music is! Like a geyser it seems to shoot
> forth out of the myth's pre-cultural depths—and not only
> seems, for it actually does it—and in very truth it is con-
> ceived, deliberately, calculatedly, with high intelligence,
> with an extreme of shrewdness, in a spirit as literary as
> the spirit of the texts is musical.   (E3D, 319–320)

In *Doctor Faustus* Leverkühn gives a more generalized
exposition of this idea for the instruction of Zeitblom who
records it thus:

> Music and speech, he insisted, belonged together, they
> were at bottom one, language was music, music was
> language; separate, one always appealed to the other,
> imitated the other, used the other's tools, always the one
> gave itself to be understood as substitute of the other. How
> music could *be* first of all word, be thought and planned
> as word, he would demonstrate to me by the fact that
> Beethoven had been seen composing in words. 'What is he
> writing there in his notebook?' it had been asked. 'He is
> composing.' 'But he is writing words, not notes.' Yes,
> that was a way he had. . . . It was very natural that music
> should take fire at the word, and that the word should
> burst forth out of music, as it did towards the end of the
> Ninth Symphony. Finally it was a fact that the whole de-
> velopment of music in Germany strove towards the word-
> tone drama of Wagner and therein found its goal. (163–4)

Mann, although not himself a composer, had other
options open to him:

> It is quite uncertain in what language I write, whether
> Latin, French, German or Anglo-Saxon [he has Brother

Clemens say for him in *The Holy Sinner*] . . . By no means
do I assert that I possess all the tongues; but they run all
together in my writing and become one—in other words,
language. . . . The spirit of narration is free to the point
of abstraction, whose medium is language in and for itself,
language itself, which sets itself as absolute and does not
greatly care about idioms and national linguistic gods.
(HS, 5–6)

'Free to the point of abstraction', 'Language in and for
itself'—here we have a theory assigning essentially
musical properties to language, although others such as
Mallarmé and Joyce went far further here in practice
than Mann ever did. The abstraction inherent in music,
and in words used as though they were musical elements,
opens up a reality which discredits and transcends the
present one; words, like music, may here speak 'in a
language which reason does not understand' (as Schopenhauer said), and how obviously attractive was such a
usage to an ironist like Mann! For it is a natural pro-
gression from the ambiguities of language in which the
ironist delights to an abstract, quasi-musical use of language. Mann's language remains verbal and specific, but
the pull towards musical abstraction is ever present. We
have perhaps here an insight into the continuing popu-
larity of music and the ascendancy of abstract tendencies
in the arts in an age wary of any kind of faith or
affirmation.

By his several uses of language and languages, Mann
is able to juggle simultaneously with several realities,
several pictures of the world. In *Doctor Faustus* we find
three contrapuntal time planes, two explicit—Zeitblom's
time of writing, and the fictional events of Leverkühn's
life that he describes and the third, latent—the ground-
bass of historical events which are sometimes alluded to

directly and sometimes fictionalized. Mann does not have to choose between these fictions and reality, and may handle them as freely as he sees fit to do. In music, where all these 'pictures', these 'games' with definable meanings, merge and are left behind, all realities may be contained and, to Mann, versed in Schopenhauer as he was, the complete abstraction reveals 'the innermost essence of the world'. For Faust to be a musician opens doors for him which, as any nineteenth-century romantic would have known, must for ever remain closed to the mere man of letters.

Mann himself was far too intelligent to abandon the limited grasp of realities offered by his verbal art in the hope of becoming a magician-musician. In *Doctor Faustus* he attacks exaltation of the risqué delights of the irrational, of musicality and the implicit depreciation of sober reason and of the surety obtained by responsible use of the Word. To make Faust a musician enables Mann to bow before the art of arts, while at the same time to criticize modern man (apparently so rational, so enlightened, so scientific) and, in particular, modern Germans, for their susceptibility to emotional persuasion. Music is a perfect example of an artefact, itself of no intrinsic moral standing, which is coloured by what we make of it. It exhibits in extreme form the indifference and moral unaccountability of great art.

But equivocal though the musical art may be, serving the powers of light and darkness without discrimination, in *Doctor Faustus* the balance is weighted on the side of darkness. Music is here for Mann, as for Nietzsche, the most indispensable and the most dangerous of the arts. Wagner, in a note to Mathilde Wesendonck, said that his *Tristan* was turning into something dreadful. He was afraid that good interpretations would drive people mad—

and his suspicions were not unfounded, as the response
of certain hypersensitive individuals to nineteenth-century *Tristan* performances confirms.* Mann was fascin-
ated by this phenomenon, and the effect of such music on
the weak and suggestible is a constant theme of his
fiction. He believed that music's demonic aspect was
apparent in that those who wrote and understood it
seemed to him to be granted insights more penetrating,
more Faustian, than those accessible to the theologian.
Hence Leverkühn's studies actually begin with theology
and from there inevitably move on into the magical,
disreputable business of music. 'Music', Mann's daughter
Monika has observed, was for her father 'necessarily
somehow linked with sin. For all that, it may be a divine
sin, and no small stimulus to his own art.'† Music shows
us what lies beneath consciousness, but, in speaking the
language of the unconscious, exercises its influence where
we are most vulnerable. The price for its intoxication of
our senses, its heightening of sensibility, is all too often
the erosion of our reserves of natural feeling. This view
of Mann's may be concisely illustrated by the epilogue to
the description of Hans Castorp's favourite records in
The Magic Mountain. (The specific reference is to
Schubert's Lindenbaum Lied from the *Winterreise* cycle.)

> At first blush [the song had seemed] proper and pious
> enough, indubitably. But the issues of it were sinister. . . .
> This was a fruit, sound and splendid enough for the instant
> or so, yet extraordinarily prone to decay; the purest
> refreshment of the spirit, if enjoyed at the right moment,
> but the next, capable of spreading decay and corruption
> among men. It was the fruit of life, conceived of death,
> pregnant of dissolution. . . .   (MM, 652)

* See, for example, Elliott Zuckerman, *The First Hundred Years
of Wagner's Tristan*, op. cit.
† Quoted in Zuckerman op. cit., p. 216.

Mann (and his characters) often speak about music in such a general, digressive sense. Typically he writes of a passage in Siegfried's funeral march: 'one scarcely knows whether it is Wagner's own peculiar and personal art, or music itself, that one so loves, that so charms one' (E3D, 321). We must take warning here and notice that when Mann refers to 'music itself', he usually has in mind Tristanesque music, like that of Hanno Buddenbrook improvising at the piano:

> an irresistible mounting, a chromatic upward struggle, a wild relentless longing, abruptly broken by startling, arresting pianissimi which gave a sensation as if the ground were disappearing from beneath one's feet, or like a sudden abandonment and sinking into a gulf of desire. (BB, 348–9)

This music is a dangerous brew concocted with consummate mastery by Wagner, and it provided Mann with what he described as his 'deepest musical experience'. He put this experience to creative use by devising literary equivalents for Wagnerian techniques so that he might emulate in his own field the musician's achievement in music. Mann freely admitted that he thought of his novels as counterparts to Wagner's operas. There can be no doubt that this essentially literary programme was a fruitful response to the Wagner whose hypnotic art had held so many subsequent musicians irredeemably in thrall. A literature which created fictions of this music's disastrous effects on those weaker than itself, afforded an exorcism of the magic. It was, after all, Mann's great merit that he upheld a rational humanism and yet never dismissed nor overlooked the creative, poetic aspects of the irrational.

CHAPTER THREE

The Political Background

Leverkühn's musicality, as we have suggested, has to do with much more than music alone. In particular it has to do with politics. That Leverkühn should be a musician is intended as a testament to German pre-eminence in matters artistic and her preference for them rather than the humdrum realities of politics, for which, according to Mann, she has little taste and rather less ability. This is perhaps indictment enough, for it is Zeitblom who concerns himself with politics, if only to the extent of passive observation, and Leverkühn not at all. In this sense, Leverkühn is errant Germany, and Zeitblom's political moralizings and exhortations are those of Mann himself. As we shall see though, Leverkühn the deliberately non-political artist and Zeitblom the responsible citizen are also projections of a personal either/or dilemma which Mann attempts to resolve in *Doctor Faustus*.

The reversal of Mann's political position from patriotic support of Germany in the First World War to open criticism of her during the Weimar Republic cannot easily be explained. In retrospect he himself found the change an embarrassment, not least because Mann the artist never fully accepted Mann the politician. The artist's proper philosophy, he believed, was that of objective detachment, admitting no allegiance other than to his own way of seeing the world. Yet he acknowledged political responsibilities and duties as a citizen, even if it was sometimes necessary for the artist to fail to believe the convictions of the responsible citizen. This conflict first becomes plain during the First World War when the artist puts aside his art and tries to meet the politician in the *Betrachtungen eines Unpolitischen* (Meditations of a Non-political Man), and it is no less pressing a quarter of a century later in *Doctor Faustus*. It is present in Zeitblom's double role as ironic, detached narrator, and, in the latter half of the novel, as scourge of Hitler's Germany.

With the coming of the First World War Mann found he could no longer hold to his preference for a 'non-political' stance. He tried to work out his difficulties in the *Meditations*, the eventual effect upon him of this being to contradict the attitude manifest in the title. He described the *Meditations* as 'the work of an artist whose existence was shaken to its foundations, whose self-respect was brought into question, and whose troubled condition was such that he was completely unable to produce anything else'.* In the *Meditations* Mann affirms the detached, aesthetic philosophy, allied as it was in his case with conservative pessimism, against committed literary politics, particularly those of republican optimism. This second position was very much that of his brother Heinrich, the *Meditations* being in many ways a polemic directed against him. Mann, however, made an unfortunate mistake in equating the cause of his conservative defence of German culture with that of Germany against her opponents in the war. To identify his own values with those of Germany led all too swiftly to a blinkered patriotism, as he later regretfully admitted. Even as late as 1953 he thought it necessary in the preface to the collection of his minor prose, *Altes und*

* Quoted in HIG, 116.

Neues, to recall 'my shame at remembering my own political folly–the polemical incomprehension with which I opposed Democracy in a certain period of my life, at the time of the First World War'.*

The progressive vehemence in Mann's denunciation of Hitler's Germany is to be measured both by the magnitude of the evil against which it was directed, and also by Mann's private need to make good his earlier political debt. The condemnations of Germany voiced by the exiled Mann in countless broadcasts and speeches, and by Zeitblom in *Doctor Faustus*, were surely sharpened by the need to make up for the insufficiently critical patriotism of the *Meditations*. As Erich Heller has well said, *Faustus* is 'a book which could only have been written by one who felt for Germany what Thomas Mann felt in 1914' (HIG, 117).

Already by 1922 Mann had changed his ideas. In a new edition of the *Meditations* he deleted many of its politically more conservative passages, and he was attacked in some quarters for so doing.† Those who had supported Mann as a champion of the old order were further put out by the lecture declaring his support for the Weimar Republic, 'Von deutscher Republik', which he gave in Berlin on October 15th, 1922 and which he called his 'republican manifesto'. By the end of the decade, his cosmopolitan horizon and critically realist view of Germany were scarcely congruent with the unlimited emotional nationalism then rife in the country. Mann's identity and feeling for the finer qualities of Germany and Germanism never deserted him, even in the years of her self-betrayal and her unrestrained plunge into the

* Quoted in HIG, 119.
† See Wesley V. Blomster, 'Thomas Mann and the Munich Manifesto', in *German Life and Letters*, January, 1969.

demonic. Her waywardness, coupled with sensitive memories of his own earlier shortcomings, only sharpened that identification and feeling. Thus, speaking in Stockholm at the time of the award of the Nobel prize in 1929, he records his pride at being honoured as a German writer:

> It is most fitting that I should lay this world prize, attached as it is to my name more or less by chance, at the feet of my country and people, this country and people with whom such as myself feel even more strongly linked today than with the time of the most radiant blossoming of her power. *

The same year sees him writing the story *Mario and the Magician*, for purposes surely as much political as artistic. It is a parable, based on Italy under Mussolini, warning against possible home dictatorship. After the Reichstag election successes of the National Socialists in September 1930, Mann delivered his 'German Address, an Appeal to Reason' in Berlin in the same Beethoven Hall where he had delivered the 1922 lecture, 'Von deutscher Republik'. He argued that the German bourgeoisie should resist National Socialism and commit themselves to the Social Democrats. This meeting was the scene of an SA demonstration from which Mann made good his escape with the help of Bruno Walter, who had a conductor's intimate knowledge of the back-stage geography of the concert hall.

Ever aware of the megalomaniacal drive in both Wagner and Hitler and the susceptibility to it of the German spirit, which was not always morally literate in such matters. Mann took good care to emphasize the grievous shortcomings of the composer. He warned

* Quoted in Blomster, op. cit., from Mann's 'Rede in Stockholm'.

against the equivocal and nationalistic appeals of his art in the lecture 'Sufferings and Greatness of Richard Wagner'* which he gave in Munich on February 10th, 1933, less than two weeks after Hitler became Reichskanzler of Germany. It would have sufficed if German audiences alone had had to listen to the unmentionable home-truths that this lecture contained; but Mann immediately embarked on a foreign lecture-tour, speaking in Amsterdam, Brussels and Paris, and this gave his political opponents the opportunity for which they had been waiting. While he was still abroad in Switzerland, forty-four leading cultural and political figures lent their signatures to an official condemnation which was printed in the *Münchner Neueste Nachrichten* in the issue of April 16/17th, 1933. It was plain to Mann that it was not safe for him to return and he reluctantly became an exile, first in Switzerland and later (from 1938) in the United States.

Extracts from Mann's journals for 1933 and 1934 (published in 1946) contain fervent denunciations of Hitler and prayers that the German people will exorcise the curse of National Socialism. In tone and substance they differ little from the later war-time broadcasts to Germany. He writes of his exile as a martyrdom 'for which I feel I was never born, but to which my spiritual dignity irresistibly calls me'. 'Hitler', he says, 'embodies to the letter the unpleasant side of Wagner, though only that much. . . . It would be a real irony of history if this most spiritual and "inward" people should be destroyed by what was originally an aristocratic and worthy clumsiness in matters of the external, actual world'.†

* This is nevertheless one of the finest appreciations of Wagner's art ever written. It is to be found in E3D.
† Quoted in GBF, 116–17.

It was not, though, until February 3rd, 1936, that Mann issued a clear statement of his condemnation of the Reich, in a letter to the Swiss literary critic Eduard Korrodi, editor of the literary supplement of the *Neue Zürcher Zeitung*. The National Socialists retaliated by depriving him of his citizenship and by stripping him of his honorary doctorate from the University of Bonn. Having freely declared his position, Mann now availed himself of every chance to attack Hitler's Germany and to warn Europe of her ambitions. In 1938 he wrote the essay 'Europe, Beware!' where he could still summon sufficient optimism to hope that Germany would be saved from an annihilating war by a new fighting humanism, which would resist and overcome the forces of barbarism.* In another essay, 'Culture and Politics', of 1939, Mann explains how he himself had once committed the fatal and typically German error of despising democracy and drawing a line between politics and the life of the mind.† He describes how he later came to realize that 'the unhappy course of German history, which has issued in the cultural catastrophe of National Socialism, is in truth very much bound up with that unpolitical cast of the bourgeois mind'. He hopes that perhaps this catastrophe will teach the German bourgeoisie the harsh lesson required to point it towards a new, politically aware, humanism.

From 1938 Mann made his home in America and from there continued, particularly in the series of fifty-five broadcasts delivered at the invitation of the BBC to Germany between 1940 and 1945, his condemnation of

---

* Quoted in GBF, 120, from *Order of the Day*: *Political Essays and Speeches of Three Decades*, translated by H. T. Lowe-Porter, E. Meyer and E. Sutton, New York, 1942.

† Quoted in GBF, 122.

the Reich and his appeals to the German people to come
to their senses. The highly charged, emotional tone of
these broadcasts is identical with that of Zeitblom's frequent condemnations of Germany in *Doctor Faustus*. In
the broadcasts Mann states his belief that Germany will
be defeated and he argues that the diabolic powers *must*
be defeated in order that a new Germany may arise.
'How bitter it is', he began the last broadcast, given on
May 10th, 1945, 'when the world is rejoicing over the
defeat, the deepest humiliation of one's own country!'*

What of Mann's hopes for the new Germany? In his
seventieth-birthday address, 'Germany and the Germans', written during a break in the work on *Faustus*,
and delivered at the Library of Congress on May 29th,
1945, he ventured to hope that the liquidation of Naz-
ism might pave the way for social reforms 'which would
offer the greatest prospect of happiness to Germany's
very inclinations and needs'. He looked forward—and
trusted that Germany would do so too—to a 'minimizing'
of political boundaries, a certain depolitization of states in
general, the awakening of mankind to a realization of
their practical unity, their first thoughts about a world
state'. At the bottom of the very loneliness that made the
German wicked, 'lay always the wish to love, the wish to
be loved. In the end the German misfortune is only the
paradigm of the tragedy of human life. And the grace
that Germany so sorely needs, my friends, all of us need
it.'† By the time he came to write *Faustus*, therefore,
Mann had long evolved a formula for smoothing the path
for the free creative play of the artist (who wrote fiction
and literary essays) by the exercise of the due political

* Quoted in GBF, 125, from *Deutsche Hörer!* 2nd ed., Stockholm,
1945.
† *Thomas Mann's Addresses*, p. 66.

responsibilities of the citizen (who wrote political speeches and essays). With quiet conscience, he could refer in *Genesis of a Novel* to 'my old habit of giving political matters equal place beside creative and personal activities, of alternating between these realms . . .' (GN, 182). An example will serve to show how this worked out in practice. He reports how in 1946, while he was working on the last part of *Doctor Faustus*,

> A crisis had risen in the United Nations over Iran and over the Anglo-American military alliance instituted by Churchill. It led to a duel of words between Churchill and Stalin. Churchill spoke with polish and Stalin coarsely; neither, I felt, was altogether wrong. This is generally my reaction, and there is only one instance in my life – and this is significant – when I have not had it. Hitler had the great merit of producing a simplification of the emotions, of calling forth a wholly unequivocal No, a clear and deadly hatred. The years of struggle against him had been morally a good era.   (GN, 131)

Mann believed too that the realms of art and politics had territory in common. Politics, he says in 'Germany and the Germans', 'actually is a realm akin to art insofar as, like art, it occupies a creatively mediating position between the spirit and life, the idea and reality, the desirable and the necessary, conscience and deed, morality and power'. *Doctor Faustus* is a product of the same reasoning, in that in it Mann attempted to heal the division of artistic and political purposes by bringing them together within the same covers – and indeed this was necessary in a work which apportions so much of the blame for the Nazi catastrophe on the political indifference of the German bourgeoisie. The German bourgeoisie were as far from democracy as they ever had been.

CHAPTER FOUR

Schoenberg and Leverkühn

Something of Schoenberg's influence on the musical aspects of Mann's book has already been described. In this chapter I shall try to show how Leverkühn's 'system' of musical composition differs in many crucial respects from Schoenberg's 12-tone Method. Schoenberg was far from pleased when he heard of the book's publication and this led to an extraordinary rift between the two men. Oddly enough, the technical discrepancies between the two compositional systems do not seem to have exercised the composer unduly.

Mann sent Schoenberg one of the first copies of the German edition, inscribing it 'Dem Eigentlichen' ("To the real one'). Although Mann clearly intended this as a compliment, Schoenberg took it quite otherwise. He was incensed to learn of the use to which Mann had put his and Adorno's musical assistance, and on three principal grounds. First, that the 12-tone Method, being his 'intellectual property', appears in the novel as Leverkühn's own invention; secondly, that while such musicians as Bruno Walter and Otto Klemperer are mentioned by name, there is no reference to himself as the rightful inventor of the 12-tone Method; and thirdly, that Leverkühn 'is depicted, from beginning to end, as a lunatic. I am now seventy-four and I am not yet insane, and I have never acquired the disease from which this insanity stems. I consider this an insult, and I might have to draw consequences.' This extract is from Schoenberg's letter in *The Saturday Review of Literature*, which brought the dispute into the light when it was published on January 1st, 1949, together with Mann's puzzled and generous reply. (The texts of both letters are reproduced in an appendix.) Schoenberg, however, had taken private exception much earlier—and before he had even read the book. According to him, he first heard about 'this abuse' when he read a review in a magazine; his attention was then drawn to it by Alma Mahler-Werfel,* and finally the inscribed copy arrived, which he still had not read by the time he came to write to *The Saturday Review*— possibly because of the 'nervous eye-affliction' given as the reason in a letter to Josef Rufer, dated May 25th, 1948.† Alma Mahler-Werfel took up the cudgels on Schoenberg's behalf. 'It was immediately clear to me', she wrote in her autobiography,‡

> that Mann had drawn extensively on Arnold Schoenberg's twelve-tone system, which he appeared to regard as commonly known and in use. When I saw him again, I praised the beauty of the novel and discreetly remarked that it had surprised me to find Schoenberg's theory so popularly and yet recognizably presented.
>
> 'So you recognized it?' Mann was slightly put out. I said no musician could fail to recognize it.
>
> 'Do you think Schoenberg will mind?' Mann asked, and I shrugged, not wanting to set off a general discussion.

---

* She was mentioned earlier (see p. 11) as having with her third husband, the writer Franz Werfel, entertained Mann and Schoenberg together in Los Angeles, and thus given the novelist the chance to consult the composer about musical technique. Born in 1879, she successively married Gustav Mahler (1902–11), the architect Walter Gropius (1915–18), and Franz Werfel (1929–45). She died in New York in 1964. Clearly something of a lion-hunter.

† *Arnold Schoenberg: Letters.*

‡ Alma Mahler-Werfel, *And the Bridge is Love*, Hutchinson, London, 1959, p. 275.

In fact, Schoenberg was outraged. Next morning he asked my help in getting Mann to print a note in the book to the effect that the theory was Schoenberg's invention. I called Mann's home. His wife answered, and at first resented the idea. I called again and again, always consulting Schoenberg in between, and after dinner Katia Mann finally promised that 'Tommy' would insert an explanation in future editions and have it pasted into copies already in print. And although the wording did not quite satisfy Schoenberg, that settled the matter.

But Schoenberg was far from satisfied, for the inserted explanation had made matters very much worse. It reads as follows:

> It does not seem supererogatory to inform the reader that the form of musical composition delineated in Chapter XXII, known as the twelve-tone or row system, is in truth the intellectual property of a contemporary composer and theoretician, Arnold Schönberg. I have transferred this technique in a certain ideational context to the fictitious figure of a musician, the tragic hero of my novel. In fact, the passages of this book that deal with musical theory are indebted in numerous details to Schönberg's *Harmonielehre*.

'Mr. Mann', said Schoenberg in *The Saturday Review*,

> was not as generous as I, who had given him good chance to free himself from the ugly aspect of a pirate. He gave an explanation: a few lines which he hid at the end of the book on a place on a page where no one ever would see it. Besides, he added a new crime to his first, in the attempt to belittle me: He calls me '*a* [a!] *contemporary* composer and theorctician'. Of course, in two or three decades, one will know which of the two was the other's contemporary.

For his part, Mann was 'astonished and grieved' when Schoenberg chose to carry the dispute so aggressively into the public arena after their personal correspondence which 'had been of a thoroughly friendly character in all

D

its phases'. He had thought Schoenberg would have been satisfied by the insertion of the explanatory note. In his letter to *The Saturday Review*, Mann stressed that Schoenberg should have been content to regard the appearance of the 12-tone Method in the novel as a tribute to his enormous influence on the era—for this musical system had long since become a part of our cultural pattern,

> used by countless composers throughout the world, all of whom have tacitly purloined it from its originator. . . . I sincerely believed that every child in our cultural area [*sic*] must at one time or another have heard about the twelve-tone system and its initiator, and that no one on earth, having read my novel, could possibly imagine that I was its inventor [such indeed was one of Schoenberg's fears] or was trying to pose as such.

As to the syphilitic theme,

> the idea that Adrian Leverkühn is Schoenberg, that the figure is a portrait of him, is so utterly absurd that I scarcely know what to say about it. There is no point of contact, not a shade of similarity, between the origin, the traditions, the character, and the fate of my musician, on the one hand, and the existence of Schoenberg on the other. 'Doctor Faustus' has been called a Nietzsche-novel, and, indeed, the book, which for good reasons avoids mention of Nietzsche's name, contains many references to his intellectual tragedy, even direct quotations from the history of his illness.

The controversy continued through 1949. Mann himself 'was absolutely determined not to increase his [Schoenberg's] hostility, but to allow it to remain one-sided and never to say a bad word about him . . .'*

---

* Letter from Mann to H. H. Stuckenschmidt, dated October 19th, 1951, published in the latter's *Arnold Schoenberg*, p. 11.

Happily it ended in January 1950, although news of the fact was not made public until after Schoenberg's death on July 13th, 1951, partly because Schoenberg had not wanted to 'stab in the back all those who supported me in this fight—friends, acquaintances, and strangers'.* Mann and Schoenberg had been united in their refusal to allow *The Saturday Review* to publish the exchange of letters in an anthology and this seems to have brought them together. At the end of 1949 Mann wrote a conciliatory letter which Schoenberg accepted as follows:

> If the hand that I believe I see held out is the hand of peace, that is, if it signifies an offer of peace, I should be the last not to grasp it at once and shake it in token of confirmation.
>
> In fact: I have often thought of writing to you and saying: Let us bury the hatchet and show that on a certain level there is always a chance of peace. . . . Let us make do with this peace: you have reconciled me.
>
> I remain, with deep regard, yours faithfully,
>
> ARNOLD SCHOENBERG.†

It is not the least of the many peculiarities of this bizarre affair that Schoenberg should have wished to be associated at all with a book in which the music has its source in syphilis and the devil—he had been told at least enough about it to have known that. Mann himself was over-ready to wash his hands of the book's 'Schoenberg content' which, although strictly limited and of lesser significance than the 'Nietzsche content', is none the less real. Leverkühn's musical system and the use he makes of it differ considerably from those of Schoenberg, as will be shown, one reason for this being that Mann deployed his *ad hoc* version to air reservations about twentieth-century music.

* Letter from Schoenberg to Mann, dated January 2nd, 1950, in *Schoenberg: Letters*, p. 278.　　　　† Ibid.

There were certainly grounds for Schoenberg's displeasure. Mann had been a frequent visitor to the Schoenbergs' house in Brentwood Park, Los Angeles, and must have questioned the Master closely on musical matters. Yet however much he admired Schoenberg the man, he certainly did not enjoy Schoenberg's music, and would seem instinctively to have distrusted its revolutionary aspect. Whatever their personal relationship may have been, Mann, spurred on as we shall see by Adorno, clearly lost no time in articulating his distrust as specifically as possible.

Adorno's admiration for Schoenberg did not prevent his being critical of Schoenberg's ideas and methods of composition and many of his doubts find their way almost unmodified into *Doctor Faustus*. Mann acknowledged Adorno's help thus: 'The analysis of the row system and the criticism of it that is translated into dialogue in Chapter XXII of *Faustus* is entirely based upon Adorno's essay' (GN, 40).*

But Mann hastens to add that he was only 'appropriating what I felt to be my own'. He had read Adorno's manuscript with a feeling of strange familiarity with its ideas and had had no hesitation in taking what he wanted from them. For, in the Adorno essay, certain

> ideas about death and form, the self and the objective world, may well be regarded by the author of a Venetian novel [*Death in Venice*] of some thirty-five years ago as recollections of himself. They could well have their place in the younger man's musicological essay and at the same time serve me in my canvas of persons and an epoch. An idea as such will never possess much personal and proprietary value in the eyes of an artist.

* The reference is to Adorno's as then unpublished *Philosophie der neuen Musik*.

Schoenberg would have been in no hurry to endorse that last notion. Mann, on the contrary, had no scruples whatever about working in any material that suited his purpose, even if it included what Schoenberg was later to describe as 'my intellectual property'–i.e., the principle of serial composition. In this pedantic respect, Schoenberg's charge of plagiarism was certainly justified.

Leverkühn is placed by Mann in very much the same historical predicament that Schoenberg found himself in, although his birth date of 1885 would make him eleven years younger than Schoenberg (and so an exact fictional contemporary of Alban Berg). As if to make up for the eleven years, Leverkühn is given a musical start on Schoenberg. Almost before he writes a single note, Leverkühn is aware of an acute artistic impasse–which Schoenberg certainly wasn't. Schoenberg did not question his inheritance until he had put it on trial and found it wanting. He worked himself into an impasse rather than took one over. He started from where Brahms and Wagner left off and his musical revolution only became a necessity when his expressive needs took him beyond the rich language of late chromatic tonality into his new world of so called free atonality. His early songs, his string sextet *Verklärte Nacht* (1899), the Straussian tone poem *Pelléas und Mélisande* (1902–3), his first string quartet (1904–5), and several other works were perfectly sincere extensions of a language which he took on its own terms and in which he believed. On the other hand, Leverkühn's first opus, his symphonic fantasy *Meerleuchten* (Ocean Lights), is 'a very remarkable instance of how an artist can give his best to a thing in which he privately no longer believes . . . a disillusioned masterpiece of *koloristischer Orchesterbrillanz* which already bore within itself the traits of parody and intellectual mockery of art, which in Leverkühn's later work so often emerged in a creative and uncanny way' (151).

The composer of *Tristan* found no cause to be shy about tonality, as witness *Die Meistersinger*, in C major and the 162 bars of E-flat major with which *Der Ring des Nibelungen* emerges from the primeval *Urwelt*. Mann makes no attempt to reconstruct the historical bridge from here to the language of free atonality which gave birth to the strict serial method of composition. Tonality, or so the devil tells Leverkühn when they meet, is now played out and so much so that tonal sounds have now inherited the power to shock that was once the prerogative of dissonance:

> Every composer of the better sort carries within himself a canon of the forbidden, the self-forbidding, which by degrees includes all the possibilities of tonality, in other words all traditional music. . . . Tonal sounds, chords in a composition with the technical horizon of today, outbid every dissonance. As such they are to be used, but cautiously and only *in extremis*, for the shock is worse than the harshest discord of old. Everything depends on the technical horizon. (239)

Now the 'new' acquires meaning only when set in or against the context of the 'old', whatever that may happen to be at the time. What the devil is really saying here, whether he means it or not, is that far from being played out, tonality has acquired a new-found eloquence. This, then, is why Leverkühn chose to set the 'darkly shocking' verses of Blake's 'Silent, silent night' ('But an honest joy/Does itself destroy/For a harlot coy') to 'very simple harmonies, which in relation to the tone-language of the whole had a "falser", more heart-rent, uncanny effect than the most daring harmonic tensions, and made one actually experience the common chord growing monstrous' (263). Another of Leverkühn's early works, the *Brentano Song Cycle*,* is intended to show that an economical style may be more effective than the rich and complex one which it follows. This *Brentano Song Cycle* could conceivably have been modelled on Schoenberg's *Pierrot Lunaire*. In *Pierrot Lunaire* Schoenberg went forward by renunciation: he abandoned the expressionist complexity and excess of such scores as *Erwartung* and *Die glückliche Hand* and sought out a means of expression less congested and more efficient. But the most striking parallel between *Pierrot* and the *Brentano Song Cycle* is that both real and fictional compositions show the rudiments of what was to be systematized later into 12-tone serial technique. Whether Mann deliberately based this aspect of the *Brentano Song Cycle* on *Pierrot* (which he must have known) remains a matter for speculation.

In *Pierrot*, the passacaglia nocturne ('Nacht') permutes one three note motif (E, G, E-flat) through more than a hundred variants in twenty six bars, harmonically, melodically, contrapuntally in every way imaginable. Leverkühn, describing the birth of his 12-tone strict style to Zeitblom, points out that 'O lieb Mädel' in the *Brentano Cycle*

> is entirely derived from a fundamental figure, a series of interchangeable intervals, the five notes B, E, A, E, E-flat, and the horizontal melody and the vertical harmony are determined and controlled by it, in so far as that is possible with a basic motif of so few notes. It is like a word, a key word, stamped on everything in the song, which it would like to determine entirely. (191)†

* Clemens Maria Brentano, 1778–1842.
† This five note series is derived somewhat loosely from one of the novel's more obvious leitmotifs (discussed here in chapter five,

This, Leverkühn continues, was but a beginning, for from here one would have to go on to use all twelve notes of the 'tempered semi-tone alphabet'. No note would henceforth appear which did not fulfil its function in the whole structure. Zeitblom, while agreeing that 'a sort of astronomical regularity and legality would be obtained', objects that the recurrence of a fixed set of intervals would probably lead to 'unavoidable serious musical impoverishment and stagnation'. Leverkühn's reply, 'Probably', is surely an opportunity seized by Mann to have his own scepticism endorsed for one moment by his hero. 'What does it matter', runs the overtone of that 'probably', 'if the 12-tone Method leads to serious musical impoverishment and stagnation – for this has surely already happened long past recall.' Leverkühn is here made to voice, perhaps ironically or disinterestedly, his agreement with a theory which he was meant to be doing his best to refute.

But it is when Leverkühn comes to describe the variant forms of the row that the difference between his 12-tone Method and Schoenberg's becomes most apparent. He maintains that 'The decisive factor is that every note, without exception, has significance and function according to its place in the basic series or its derivatives': this 'would guarantee what I call the indifference to harmony and melody' (192); the emancipation of the dissonance 'would warrant any combination of notes which can be explained in terms of the system' (193). This is a travesty of the Schoenbergian concept of the row. Schoenberg's idea was that because every note stuck to its own pre-arranged place in the row, it therefore bore an entirely

---

p. 71), the name which Leverkühn gave to his infected harlot–
H (the note B in German) EtAEra Es (= E-flat) meralda.

specific relation to the musical 'space' as a whole, whose dimensions both of melody and harmony were mapped out by the row. Whatever the drift of the composition, the individual note could not help but be precisely related, melodically and harmonically, to all the other notes of the series.

Schoenberg, however, insisted that it was no good trying to compose with twelve notes 'related only to each other' if the composer were anything short of fluent in his handling of the classical tonal and late romantic chromatic styles. He once said that composition with the 12-tone Method penalized the composer, 'for composing thus does not become easier, but rather ten times more difficult'. What Schoenberg meant by this was that one had to be aware of all the ways a note might be heard in the revolving constellation. It was not at all sufficient that, say, the resultant 'harmony' had to be accepted as 'right' once the note had been placed satisfactorily with regard to melodic and contrapuntal requirements. The demands of the row were not to be considered as taking precedence over all the other demands, whether technical or expressive, of a well-made composition.

*   *   *

Zeitblom doubts whether the unifying complexities of 12-tone construction will be apparent to the listener. 'Do you hope to have people hear all that?' (192), he asks. Leverkühn replies that he would not expect the 'precise realization in detail' to be followed completely. What would be heard would be not the means but only the end, the achievement of 'the highest and strictest order', the perception of which would afford an 'unknown aesthetic satisfaction'.

Schoenberg would neither have disowned nor denied

the possibility of an aesthetic satisfaction from perceiving, even perhaps unconsciously, a hierarchical order beyond and above the contribution of the individual bar. This, however, he would not have regarded as any more remarkable than awareness of the home key in a piece of classical tonal music.

For Schoenberg, composition with the twelve tones had no other aim than to maintain 'comprehensibility' in a music more complex than any ever written before. 'The artistic value', he said, 'demands comprehensibility, not only for intellectual, but also for emotional satisfaction.'*

*   *   *

The difference between Leverkühn's fictional theory of a 12-tone system and Schoenberg's Method is thus considerable. The real Method evolved slowly over a wide span of Schoenberg's mature development, while Leverkühn's theory appears quite suddenly—as an idea whose details are reasoned out, and the whole put into practice, forthwith. In Schoenberg's progress from the Two Songs Op. 1 of 1896–98 to the first 12-tone compositions, which date from 1923, the common chord is allowed no time in which to grow monstrous: the frenzied expressive need urges the music forward through the extreme limits of tonality into free atonality. We see Schoenberg struggling to work out his ideas and being forced to accept that they required a new language for their expression. In a programme note provided in 1909 for the first performance of the Stefan George song cycle, *Das Buch der hängenden Gärten* (The Book of the Hanging Gardens) composed the previous year, he said: 'I am following an inner compulsion that is stronger than education, and

* *Style and Idea,* p. 103.

am obeying a law that is natural to me, and therefore stronger than my artistic training.'

This was fifteen years before the first 12-tone works.

It is Schoenberg's 'compulsion' that is so striking, the seething cauldron of ideas—compare Leverkühn, with his arrogant distaste, his dominant feeling of parody. The Method was crucial to Leverkühn in that without it he found it impossible to compose anything *serious*—it was more a means of beginning than (as it was with Schoenberg) of carrying on.

For Schoenberg the Method might partly have been considered as a resistance with which to discipline a music which had become increasingly dictated by uncontrollable, unconscious forces. Yet it was something thrown up by the music itself; something round which he had been feeling, without being able to discern it precisely. And when the outlines of the new discipline began to appear one can imagine with what rigorous self-questioning and caution he tested it. The eight years between the *Four Orchestral Songs* (1913–15) and the *Five Piano Pieces* of 1923 (the fifth of which is the first 12-tone work) were largely unproductive, and not wholly on account of the war, in which Schoenberg served intermittently between the end of 1915 and the end of 1917. It was a period of withdrawal, self-examination, and of one large uncompleted work of 'trial', *Die Jakobsleiter*, in which, as Webern put it, Schoenberg 'tied himself not to 12 notes but to seven'.*

Schoenberg knew that the new path was bound to be of unprecedented difficulty. The guide was to be the 12-tone Method, not as the inspiration of a moment, but

* *The Path to the New Music*, edited by Willi Reich, translated by Leo Black, Theodore Presser and Universal Edition, Pennsylvania, 1963, p. 41.

as a rationalization of what he had previously been trying
to do. Replying in a letter of 1932 to a query about
'a new manner of composition', he wrote,

> I can only refer you to my compositions published since
> about 1921. I do not know, as yet, the theoretical basis for
> these; on the purely compositional side, I must depend
> entirely on feeling, sense of form, and musical instinct. *

While Leverkühn forswears feeling, Schoenberg puts it
before all else. For Schoenberg there was no question of
anything having to justify itself before a system blessed by
'the emancipation of the dissonance'. The Method
(Schoenberg rejected the word 'system') provided an inspirational discipline, and if the music you wanted to
write was not possible within it, then that particular technique probably wasn't right for you anyway, hence no
doubt his unwillingness to teach it. The emancipation of
the dissonance is after all no historical *fait accompli* but
has to be won anew by each composer for his own style.
For Schoenberg there wasn't all that much to emancipate
anyway, 'the difference between dissonances and consonances is a gradual one . . . dissonances are the more
remote consonances . . .'†

In a letter to his brother-in-law, Rudolf Kolisch,
written in 1932, Schoenberg insists that the aesthetic
qualities of a piece cannot be deduced from analysis of
the rows:

> I cannot warn often enough against the over-valuation of
> these analyses, since they lead only to what I have always
> fought against–the recognition of how the piece is *made*;
> whereas I have always helped my students to recognize–
> what it *is*! I have tried and tried to make that comprehen-

* In Joseph Rufer, *The Works of Arnold Schoenberg*, p. 141.
† Ibid, p. 143, from Schoenberg's *Harmonielehre* (1911).

sible to Wiesengrund and also to Berg and Webern. But
they do not believe me.*

It was of course the same Wiesengrund (Adorno) who
was largely responsible for the musical substance of this
chapter of *Doctor Faustus* although, as we have seen,
Mann was only too ready to endorse his adviser's critique
of his teacher. Adorno's critique was that, however
Schoenberg might try to talk himself out of it, the
12-tone Method handed over too much artistic responsibility to the wheel of fortune. But in adopting this argument, Mann undermines it by misrepresenting the
Method, for Leverkühn's 12-tone Method is a recipe for
that very hierarchical order which Schoenberg condemned. Mann hints that Leverkühn's discovery of the
Method invited the emancipation of unreason (i.e., the
pact with the devil, struck in 1912, some two years after
Leverkühn's first 12-tone attempts), by permitting it to
run wild within some arbitrarily adopted discipline. Once
the disciplinary frame had been set up, the music, which
no longer needed to generate a developing form, could
be poured forth freely from the unconscious without any
further censorship or conscious control. Content would
not determine form, which would be provided by the
pre-arranged order of the Method.

This, for Mann, was the ultimate artistic (and of
course, political) folly. Zeitblom speaks for him:

> The rationalism you call for has a good deal of superstition
> about it— of belief in the incomprehensibly and vaguely
> daemonic, the kind of thing we have in games of chance,
> fortune-telling with cards, and shaking dice. Contrary to
> what you say, your system seems to me more calculated to
> dissolve human reason in magic.   (193)

* In Joseph Rufer, *The Works of Arnold Schoenberg*, p. 141.

This is none other than Adorno's critique of Schoenberg —the subjection of music to rigorous rational analysis effecting the very converse of rationality. The point was, said Mann (paraphrasing Adorno), that 'over the head of the artist, as it were, the art is cast back into a dark, mythological realm' (GN, 40).

Leverkühn replies to Zeitblom by carrying his closed hand to his brow: 'Reason and magic', he says, 'may meet and become one in that which one calls wisdom, initiation; in belief in the stars, in numbers . . .' (194). And there he trails off in distaste and pain, for reason can serve his argument no further.

*   *   *

Just as Leverkühn himself is not at all intended as a totally black figure, so his 12-tone Method is described as having positive qualities, chief among which is the idea that freedom is to be found only within discipline. Naturally, the more extreme the expressive impulse, the stricter the style necessary for its artistic transformation. As André Gide wrote about Bach's *Art of Fugue*:

> . . . one does not often feel in it either serenity or beauty, but rather an intellectual torment and an effort of the will to bend forms as rigid as laws and inhumanly inflexible. It is the triumph of the mind over figures; and, before the triumph, the struggle. And while submitting to restraint— through it, in spite of it, or *thanks to it*—all the play of emotion, of tenderness, and, after all, of harmony that can still remain. *

Or consider a typical statement by Schoenberg's pupil Webern in a letter of August 6th, 1943, to Willi Reich:

> I've completed another piece as part of the plan I've told

---

* *Journals, 1889–1949*, entry of December 7th, 1921, translated by Justin O'Brien, Penguin edition, Harmondsworth, 1967, p. 336.

you of several times; a bass aria. It's all even stricter, and for that reason it's also become still freer.*

Just how far disciplinary strictness should be pushed in a totalitarian direction was a question which caused some anxiety to the politically conscious Mann. He seems to have believed that there was something unusually culpable in rigid adherence to the 12-tone Method. But there is nothing that sets serial discipline apart in kind from the very many other unifying formal disciplines and techniques followed by composers through the centuries. The fugue, for example, has long been valued as a disciplinary form par excellence. It provides at once a technical 'game' to stimulate the free-ranging imaginative faculties, and an aesthetically satisfying shape to the whole.

Another positive aspect of Leverkühn's adoption of the 12-tone Method is revealed when Zeitblom asks what would happen if 'the *Konstellation* produced the banal: consonance, triad harmony, the worn-out, the diminished seventh?' Leverkühn replies that this would be 'a renewal of the worn-out by the *Konstellation*'. In the 1920s Schoenberg would have denied this; he said that any accidental reminiscence of tonal harmony was to be carefully avoided because it might upset the precarious new 12-tone democracy. But although it is doubtful whether he ever formally withdrew this prohibition, several of his works of the 1930s and 1940s show that the renewal could and did occur. His pupil Alban Berg said straight out in 1929 that 'if . . . something tonal is included in twelve-note composition, that would be a great gain from the musical side'.† Berg was indeed able

* Webern, *The Path to the New Music*, op. cit., p. 64.
† Willi Reich, *Alban Berg*, Thames and Hudson, London, 1965, p. 79.

to achieve this (as, for instance, in the Violin Concerto, with its tonally orientated series, and in many other works) – and all his music is evidence of a lifelong interest in reconciling tonality with serial composition. But it is worth emphasizing that for Berg there was no question that the *Konstellation* might accidentally rejuvenate tonality. The new life for tonality was hammered out in full deliberation *via* the 12-tone Method. Any idea of the accidental rejuvenation of the commonplace through the Method is highly suspect. Schoenberg, Berg and Webern had the strongest views about the music they were each trying to write with the aid of the Method; Leverkühn places absolute trust in the row and is ready to defend whatever music may ensue.

We may conclude, therefore, that although Mann worked in certain theoretical ideas derived from Schoenberg, the end result should be described, as Schoenberg himself once described it, as 'Leverkühn's 12-Tone Gulash [*sic*]'. Whatever Mann's intentions may have been – and his own statements do not completely elucidate them – the fact is that he adapts Schoenberg's idea for his own novelistic purposes and does not give a true picture of it. Schoenberg's Method was purposely evolved over a long period. Leverkühn's springs much more readily to birth, and his 'serious' (as opposed to ironic or parodistic) music only appears with it. For Schoenberg, the Method was a natural musical law, as natural as tonality, which could be used for writing a music more concentrated and expressive than ever before. For Leverkühn, the Method was a demonic, magical device, served and worshipped by the music it brought forth.

CHAPTER FIVE

Education of a Faust

Doctor Faustus opens slowly, almost pedantically. This allows Mann a leisurely exposition of his leitmotifs, and gives him time to build up a complex rapport between the reader and his narrator, Zeitblom. There will be more to say later about the measure of Mann's identification with Zeitblom, but, in the Zeitblom of the opening chapters, his use of the character for an elaborate exercise in self-mockery is particularly striking.

Zeitblom begins by introducing himself. He is seated at his desk on May 23rd, 1943, which we learn is some three years after Leverkühn's death; and we know that it was on this day, too, that Mann began to write the novel. Zeitblom immediately alludes to the demonic nature of his theme which, he assures us, has always been alien to *his* nature. The demonic has even been responsible for his early resignation of his 'beloved teaching profession'—this being a transparent autobiographical reference to Mann's decision to leave Germany rather than compromise himself in any way with National Socialism.

Zeitblom introduces us to the young Leverkühn, born in 1885 at the prosperous family estate at Buchel, near Kaisersaschern, and we quickly learn of his irrepressible sense of the ridiculous. His father Jonathan is a dedicated student of the natural sciences, to whom such freakish phenomena as oil-drops which can be induced to behave as amoeba, and chemicals which can simulate plant life,

E

are sources of religious awe. To his son Adrian, a soul baptized to total scepticism, they are little more than proofs of the fatuity of attempting to draw too fine a line between appearance and reality.* This notion is loosely derived from Nietzsche who, Mann liked to point out, had himself taken over from Schopenhauer the idea that life was to be justified only as an aesthetic phenomenon. Art and appearance were all, since life was based upon deception, perspective and illusion. Error, Nietzsche had believed, was the source of all vitality (LE, 151). Mann puts this idea on trial in Leverkühn, for his fictional composer's mature music owes its 'inspired' vitality to a syphilitic infection: the healthy organism is undermined by syphilis so that it will be the more productive in unhealth. The osmotic chemical process by which the infection is to infiltrate the composer's nervous system is prefigured, leitmotif style, in that we are told that it was osmosis which was responsible for the phenomena of the animate behaviour of the inanimate which had so impressed Father Jonathan.

Jonathan, we may well believe, would have held that mysteries of appearance and reality are attributable to the wisdom of the Divine Order, while Adrian would have found that idea absurd. To the modern, psychological mind there can be no easy demarcation between appearance and reality: both may be equally unreal. It is all a diabolical jest and the one touchstone of ultimate reality is the persistence of doubt.

Leverkühn is allowed nothing whatever of that naive spontaneity which has helped others to gain their 'necessary little ascendancy over the impediments of unbelief, arrogance, and intellectual self-consciousness' (152). He

* Using these words as descriptions of phenomena, rather than in their Platonic sense.

offers no lament for the lost life-force and is content to
work out his own substitute for it. 'I'd like to know', he
confides to Zeitblom,

> whether epochs that were really cultured knew the word
> at all, or used it. Naïveté, unconsciousness, taken-for-
> grantedness, seems to me to be the first criterion of the
> constitution to which we give this name. What we are
> losing is just this naïveté, and this lack . . . protects us
> from many a colourful barbarism which altogether per-
> fectly agreed with culture. . . . We should have to become
> very much more barbaric to be capable of culture again.
> (59–60)

This association of culture with barbarity is another
Nietzschean notion. Nietzsche held that culture could
only be renewed by strong doses of barbarity; it was vain
sentimentalism to expect anything in the way of culture
and greatness from men if they had lost the urge to go to
war. This was an aspect of Nietzsche's thought to which
Mann often drew critical attention,* and it is an unmistakably Nietzschean Leverkühn who suggests that, if
naive spontaneity were ever to regain the 'necessary little
ascendancy', then a sustained attack on the domination
of the intellect would be required. Mann himself believed that, for all modern man's self-consciousness, reason
and intellect were to be zealously asserted against the
totally unproductive barbarism which was bound to erupt,
and had indeed done so, should the primitive instinctual
forces be allowed to run away with themselves. His
point, as will become clearer later on, is that a strategy
which might have some validity in art is disastrous if
practised in the world of everyday reality.

*   *   *

* See, for instance, LE, 164.

We learn something of Leverkühn's mother, of her vigour and simplicity, of her beautiful voice, and of the boy's early lessons in part-singing. The lessons, though, come not from her, for she 'refrained, in a sort of chaste reserve, from song', but from Hanne, the stable girl, 'this creature smelling of her animals' who sings, lustily and unashamedly, songs 'mostly either gruesome or mawkish' (23). In Hanne, Mann personifies his belief in music's inherent animality. The idea is that Leverkühn's first decisive encounter with music should be in this form rather than in the more sophisticated and responsible version which he might have acquired from his mother, had she been willing.

The part-singing episode also suggests a cultural discontinuity of no less an order than that between Adrian and his father. Hanne's lusty fluency is contrasted with a Tiresias-like silence born of prophetic knowledge and finer feeling. One can readily understand how such a silence might be the proper response not only to such culpably innocent music-making as Hanne's, but also to the blunted German language—the result of the brutally efficient completion in the Third Reich of a corrosive process that had already set in. The vitality of language is the measure of culture. As Mann well knew, the efforts of such people as the influential Viennese satirist Karl Kraus had been woefully inadequate in the defensive fight to construct an effective 'drainage system for the broad marshes of phraseology'.* We are hardly surprised that Zeitblom should list the confusion between words and ideas as a reason for his early retirement:

* This was Kraus's declared strategy against the linguistic abuses of literature, politics, and the press in his journal *Die Fackel* (The Torch), 1899–1936. Quoted in Frank Field, *The Last Days of Mankind: Karl Kraus and his Vienna*, Macmillan, London, 1967, p. 18.

within himself whatever laws he can discover. What
sense can there be in an immanent demonology, other
than the acceptance of irrationality and disorder as laws
in their own right? If order and reason are not to be
obtained without sacrifice of self, then the self must set to
work and create its own order, even if in the process it
must needs laugh, both to disguise the nature of the deed
and to comfort itself against it. Leverkühn has no
intuition that religion, through loss of respect for the devil,
might, unknowingly, become demonology. Although
prepared in the event to argue bitterly with his devil and
to spurn him, he comes to respect the devil, and to accept
his solution as the only one left. Conscious of neglected
demonic possibilities, he toys with the idea of dropping
academic theology and making something of his musical
inclinations.

Writing to Kretschmar, he wrestles against himself to
test the strength of his musical vocation. In his 'confession in avoidance' he pleads that his nature is not that
of the artist, and that his is a 'quickly satisfied intelligence';
robust naïveté, warmth, joy, love and affirmation of life
are quite foreign to him. He speaks of his sense of satiety
being stronger than that of opportunity, and confesses
that the mysterious and wonderful seem to him to be
merely ridiculous. 'I fled from this exaggerated sense of
the comic into theology, in the hope that it would give
relief to the tickling—only to find there too a perfect
legion of ludicrous absurdities' (134).

In his reply Kretschmar says he 'would leave the
question open, how far Adrian was accusing himself in
order to excuse his corresponding accusations against
art . . .' and goes on to argue that the reasoning which
Adrian sees as necessitating his avoidance of music is, on
the contrary, precisely that which should commit him

to music. 'The coolness, the "quickly satisfied intelligence", the eye for the stale and absurd, the early
fatigue, the capacity for disgust—all that was perfectly
calculated to make a profession of the talent bound up
with it' (134–5). These failings, Kretschmar insists, are
not only personal but are representative of the state of
the true province of art, of the *collective* itself. ' . . . the
coming of the new addresses itself to whatever vehicle
has the strongest subjective sense of the staleness, fatuity
and emptiness of the means still current. . . . I tell you
that the will to life and to living, growing art puts on the
mask of these faint-hearted personal qualities to manifest
itself therein, to objectivate, to fulfil itself.'

And so the decision is made and at the beginning of the
winter term 1905, Leverkühn moves from Halle to the
University of Leipzig, where Kretschmar is now living
(and where Nietzsche had studied classical philology), to
resume, with renewed seriousness, the musical studies
which he had been unable to put aside any longer.

There Leverkühn writes his first works, the most notable of which, the symphonic fantasy *Meerleuchten*, is
not only an exercise in insincerity, as has been mentioned in the previous chapter (p. 43), but is also,
strangely enough for a German composer of his vintage,
an impressionistic exercise after the manner of Debussy
and Ravel. Leverkühn next sets sections of the *Purgatorio* and *Paradiso* of Dante. He chooses 'the frightfully
stern sequence of verses which speak of the condemnation
of innocence and ignorance . . .' (162). These verses
speak of the rejection of the human 'in favour of an
unattainable absolute foreordination'—and Zeitblom the
humanist who, having taken up his first school-teaching
appointment in Kaisersaschern, has not seen his friend
for some years, is much angered when he learns that

Adrian has chosen to set such lines. Not until his setting of the parable in the *Purgatorio* of the man with a light at his back, which lights only the path of those coming after, does Leverkühn earn the undesired forgiveness of his bewildered and well-meaning friend.

*   *   *

Now that the musical decision has been taken, there remains one crucial determinant to set Leverkühn irreversibly on his path—the syphilitic infection. As mentioned before, this episode is modelled on an adventure that befell the young and ascetic Nietzsche, who had fled from the brothel to which a guide in Cologne had taken him when he had asked for a hotel. It is sometimes suggested that Nietzsche later returned to another brothel where he was equal to the demands of the occasion, thereby catching the syphilis which was to lead to an atypical general paresis and to his eventual insanity. Although there are some grounds for this explanation, the circumstances of Nietzsche's infection are not known with any certainty.* Mann accepted the story of the second brothel visit† and transposed both visits into Leverkühn's biography.

* See Walter Kaufmann's introduction, p. 13, in NK, and for a fuller account, the same author's *Nietzsche*, Princeton University Press, 1950, and subsequent editions.

† In 'Nietzsche's Philosophy in the Light of Recent History', an essay written at the time of *Doctor Faustus*, Mann quotes evidence to the effect that Nietzsche himself had told the clinic at Basle that he had been specifically infected twice in previous years. Mann also points out that the medical history preserved at Jena gives the year 1866 for the first of these misadventures. In other words [Mann speculates] one year after he had fled from the house in Cologne he returned—without diabolic guidance [Mann said he had always considered the guide who had led Nietzsche to the first brothel 'as a kind of devil's emissary']—to some similar place and contracted the disease (some say deliberately, as self-punishment) which was to destroy his life but also to intensify it enormously. (LE, 145–6)

On the evening of his first day in Leipzig, after a guided tour of the city by 'a base churl . . . with a strap round his waist, a red cap and a brass badge and a rain-cape . . .' (141) Leverkühn is led unwittingly to a brothel. The virgin composer attempts to escape the flesh (just as Nietzsche had said *he* had done) by taking refuge at the keyboard of the conveniently open house piano (to resolve a pressing harmonic problem, Leverkühn would have Zeitblom understand), and then, when a dark-coloured girl brushes his cheek with her arm, 'the trauma of contact with soulless instinct' is decisive and he flees the 'lust-hell' altogether.

One particularly notices his first shocked recognition of the dark instinctive forces slumbering within *himself* which the encounter has revealed to him. By his flight to the piano he tries to prove that the mind is all; his reaction to the girl's provocation proves that it is not.

A year later, guided by the fates, he seeks out this same Esmeralda, follows her to Pressburg (on a journey taking in a visit to the Austrian première, at Graz, of Strauss's *Salome*)* and even when she warns him of her disease, he will not be dissuaded. Thus is his 'deep, deeply mysterious longing for daemonic conception' (155) fulfilled. The appearance of a 'local affection' some weeks later takes him to physicians picked from the telephone directory. But the course of treatment with the first is interrupted by the doctor's sudden death, with the second by the doctor's arrest on some unspecified charge, and Leverkühn, as if heeding a warning, gives the whole thing up. Shortly after, the local affection heals itself,

---

* Leverkühn was in good company. The Graz première in 1906 (it had to be in Graz because the 'scandalous' text had meant that it could not be given in Vienna) was attended by, among other progressive musicians, Schoenberg, Mahler, Zemlinsky and Berg. See Willi Reich, *Alban Berg*, op. cit., p. 20.

apparently of its own accord. Zeitblom and Leverkühn go to hear the Schaff-Gosch Quartet play Beethoven's Op. 132, the late quartet with the Lydian mode 'Song in Thanksgiving to God of a Convalescent' for his return to health. This slow movement had made an earlier famous ironical appearance in *Point Counter Point* (1928), which Mann had probably read as he was a great admirer of Aldous Huxley.

Nevertheless, as is later made plain, the poison had taken root in his system; in like manner a musical derivative (B, E, A, E, E-Flat) of *Hetaera esmeralda,* * as Leverkühn had called his girl, is to make frequent, if as frequently disguised, appearances in his subsequent compositions. But there had been no mimicry here, no ambiguity between appearance and reality; for the gorgeous butterfly had freely declared herself, and when the predator had swept the warning aside, had given herself to him with all the skills her art commanded.

Understandably enough, it was this incident which, perhaps above all others, was to provoke Schoenberg's wrath when the book came to be published. Ascribing to Leverkühn the invention of the 12-tone Method, *his*

* The name of a South American butterfly of the genus *Morphos* described by the English naturalist H. W. Bates in his *The Naturalist on the River Amazons* (see GBF, 51). This butterfly, as Adrian's father Jonathan had been well aware, exhibits the phenomenon known as Batesonian mimicry. Certain butterflies signal their inedibility or other danger to intending predators by a vulgar gorgeousness of hue. Other perfectly edible varieties cunningly take advantage of this warning system by mimicking the inedible variety and decking themselves out in equally gorgeous apparel.

'Hetaera' is from the Greek *hetaira* = female companion, and specifically used of 'one of a class of professional female entertainers and prostitutes in ancient Greece' (Webster's *Third New International Dictionary*). The whole name whether as poisonous, gorgeous butterfly, as infected prostitute, or as musical theme (symbolizing sensual temptation and the pact with the devil), is one of the most telling and frequently occurring leitmotifs in *Doctor Faustus*.

F

(Schoenberg's) intellectual property, was bad enough, but to suggest that it was the conception of a diseased, syphilitic mind was outrageous. As we have already seen, although Mann's intentions with respect to the 12-tone Method remain cloudy, his letter to *The Saturday Review* confirms that Leverkühn the man is certainly not intended to be modelled on Schoenberg.

*   *   *

As Mann sets the Hetaera episode *before* the dialogue with the devil—which Leverkühn concludes by sealing his demonic pact—one has the immediate impression that it is the syphilis which is the cause of the pact. However, such a reading somewhat undermines the force of the story as a whole, in much the same way that some early versions of the Faust legend attach too much importance to the pact and too little to the hero's struggle against his original demonic inclinations. This particular fault, though, is not found in Mann's version, for the description of Leverkühn's upbringing makes his demonic calling amply plain. It was predictable that Leverkühn would sooner or later put his vocation to the test. The seeking out of the syphilis is the crucial thing, not the effect that the disease has on him, for this is merely the consummation of what was there, and fully matured within him, already. Mann shrewdly pointed out in his 1933 essay on Wagner, that the love potion, seeming cause of the love and of the ensuing tragedy of Tristan and Isolde, might as well have been water. For, said Mann, the chemistry is of no account; what matters is that the lovers *believe* that they have tasted the drink of death, and are therefore free in their last minutes to defy the prohibitive code of honour by declaring their long suppressed passion. That Mann took the trouble to

emphasize this point is surely evidence that he wished
the syphilis in *Faustus* to be understood not as a first
cause but as secondary, just as he regarded National
Socialism as the flowering of a seed already ripe within
the German soul.

The syphilis is the physical sign of Leverkühn's diseased personality. In Mann's 'picture of the artist', the
syphilis represents the 'disease' which sets a man apart
and produces art; in the same way that artistic activity
is a pathological realization of 'normal' human energies,
so venereal disease is a dark attribute of love. In Mann's
political perspective, National Socialism was a warped
manifestation of a perfectly proper love of Germany, and
of pride in national traditions.

It does, therefore, seem strange that Mann places
Leverkühn's formal sealing of his pact with the devil
after, rather than before the Hetaera episode. It weakens
the development of Leverkühn's personality to have him
commit himself resolutely to his fate in the shape of an
infected prostitute's embrace, and then only afterwards
allow him to wrestle with the hazards of so doing in a
lengthy dispute between his godly and demonic selves.
(Zeitblom says he is sure that the document recording
the dialogue which immediately precedes the pact with
the devil dates from one of Leverkühn's two Italian
years, i.e., certainly after the decisive second visit to
Hetaera.) Fortunately the dialogue, with its idea of a
freely, but most painfully, chosen pact, is such a superbly
worked out invention that it eclipses the Hetaera episode.
It may even, perhaps, not be taking too great a liberty
with Mann's intentions to suppose, contra the novel's
explicit time-scheme, that Leverkühn's closely argued
debate with destiny takes place before the fatal visit
to Hetaera, and ideally between his first and second

encounters with her. Resisting any such recreative temptation, it is important that the physiological affliction
should be seen primarily as symptomatic of Leverkühn's
thoroughly demonic nature.

                    *   *   *

On visiting his friend in Leipzig after he had been
settled there a year, Zeitblom notices a new look in his
eye: 'Mute, veiled, musing, aloof to the point of offen-
siveness, full of a chilling melancholy, it ended in a
smile, with closed lips, not unfriendly, yet mocking, and
with that gesture of turning away, so habitual, so long
familiar to me' (163). But none the less, and possibly
because he was unable or unwilling to interest his new
friend Schildknapp, a translator and enthusiastic Anglo-
phile, in his project for an opera on *Love's Labour's Lost*,
he takes Zeitblom in with him as librettist. Zeitblom
notes Leverkühn's growing preoccupation with the Word
and the various ways it could be linked with, or incor-
porated into, the musical texture. He sees the attraction
of the Shakespearean subject for Leverkühn, with all its
various possibilities for parody and for making mockery of
humanism. 'He [Leverkühn] spoke with enthusiasm of
the theme, which gave opportunity to set the loutish and
"natural" alongside the comic sublime and make both
ridiculous in each other' (164). *Love's Labour's Lost* is
turned by Leverkühn into an anti-Wagnerian opéra
bouffe 'in a spirit of the most artificial mockery and
parody of the artificial: something highly playful and
highly precious: its aim the ridicule of affected asceticism
and that euphuism which was the social fruit of classical
studies' (164). From Shakespeare, Leverkühn borrows
the idea of a learned over-refinement, contemptuous of
life and nature, which sees the barbaric 'precisely in life

and nature, in directness, humanity, feeling'. Here, 'feeling came off no better than the arrogant foreswearing of it'. To put it more plainly, the opera is an anti-romantic reaction, something like the sort of thing that Hindemith had in mind in some of his early works, and we are perhaps intended to recall Hugo Wolf's obsession with comic-opera projects. As for the music, described as 'in strict chamber-music style, a delicate airy filigree, a clever parody in notes, ingenious and humoristic, rich in subtle, highly spirited ideas', this calls to ear something like the prologue to Strauss's *Ariadne auf Naxos*. Further description of Leverkühn's *Love's Labour's Lost* as 'an art for art's sake . . . an art for artists and connoisseurs . . . mixing into its ravishment a grain of hopelessness, a drop of melancholy' reminds one even more forcibly of *Ariadne* with its fine-spun thread of the Ariadne and Bacchus theme deftly interwoven with the coarser fibres of the *Commedia dell'arte*.

Leverkühn also worked on many settings of Verlaine and Blake in the original languages, and, as with the opera, without the slightest concern for the German pro vincial public; ' . . . he altogether declined to imagine a contemporary public for his exclusive, eccentric, fantastic dreams' (165). His dislike of his own very Germanness 'took the two disparate forms of a cocoonlike withdrawal from the world and an inward need for world-wideness', although as Mann very pointedly confesses elsewhere, 'German citizenship of the world was always something different from cosmopolitanism'.

The Blake settings include 'The Poison Tree', 'Silent Silent Night' (with its harlot reference), 'I saw a chapel all of gold' (which poem almost definitively evokes Leverkühn's own growing terror, his horror of pollution, and his eventual renunciation of humanity, following the poet's own after the serpent's desecration of the Host upon the altar–'So I turned into a sty/And laid me down among the swine')–and, of course, 'The Sick Rose ("O Rose, thou art sick!/The invisible worm/That flies in the night, /In the howling storm,/Has found out thy bed . . .").'

Leverkühn's last work prior to his pact with the devil is the *Brentano Song Cycle*, one of whose songs, 'O lieb Mädel', as we saw in the last chapter, is the harbinger of his new strict 12-tone style—its music is entirely derived from a 5-note figure based, significantly enough, on the letters of Hetaera's name. This song cycle is the nostalgic, almost guilty, regression to childlike sensibility of a mind embittered by the frustrations of its every attempt to break new ground. The music of the cycle, we are to understand, is ironic in its treatment of tonality and is 'at once a mockery and a glorification of the fundamental'. But the world of childhood and of naïveté tempered into artistry is still felt to be within reach. It is the world of Mahler's *Das Knaben Wunderhorn* and of Schumann's *Kinderszenen*, but with sinister prophetic overtones of Schoenberg's *Pierrot Lunaire*, for the *Brentano Song Cycle* is described as 'these dreams of a child-world and folk-world which yet are forever floating off, not to say degenerating, into the supernatural and spectral'. One of the poems, the 'Die lustigen Musikanten', is a testament to the pathos of the boy who 'early broke his leg'. Lest the point should pass too lightly, one of the early performances of the cycle made use of a boy who was 'unfortunately really crippled, using a crutch, little Jacob Nagli. He had a voice pure as a bell, that went straight to the heart' (184). Again we notice the blurring of the frontiers of art and life and the confusion of appearance and reality.

In the *Brentano Cycle* we are to see a glorification of

the fundamental—a struggle to win back the lost dimension of consonance, of true simplicity, of direct, sincere
expression, free from subversive irony and parody:

> The artistic effect [of the *Brentano Cycle*] . . . appears
> like a cultural paradox, which by inversion of the natural
> course of development, where the refined and intellectual
> grow out of the elementary, the former here plays the
> role of the original, out of which the simple continually
> strives to wrest itself free. (183)

While the composition of the *Brentano Cycle* is under way
there is much talk of the necessity of organization in art,
and Leverkühn outlines to Zeitblom his embryonic ideas
for a 12-tone discipline to take over where the major—
minor key system had broken down, due to erosions of
extreme chromaticism and rapid modulation. On leaving
Leipzig in September 1910, Leverkühn first returns to
his parents' home at Buchel for a short while and then
goes to Munich and lodges with a senator's widow named
Rodde,* in whose salon he meets the violinist Rudolf
Schwerdtfeger, a fun-loving, emotional Mephistophellan
character who courts Leverkühn's attention without
much by way of reciprocation from the latter.

Leverkühn's longing to go back and begin again from
some point safely prior to that at which an apparently
irreversible complexity set in, is fulfilled, at least in
down-to-earth terms, in that he eventually finds a place
for his life's work which, even down to the farm dog, is a
replica of the home where he grew up. He had first seen
the Schweigestill farm at Pfeiffering† near Waldshut

---

* A partial portrait of Mann's mother, Julia, see GBF, 20.

† This is a good example of the way Mann invokes the resonance
of previous versions of the Faust story. In the first Faust chapbook
'Pfeiffering' is the name of the hamlet where Faust, in best Till
Eugenspiegel style, deceives the horse-coper with a bundle of straw.
See also footnote on p. 104 for Pfeiffering's 'true' location.

while on a bicycling expedition with his friend Rüdiger Schildknapp, although the conscious decision to live there is not taken until he has sealed his pact with the devil. (Do we perhaps detect in the name 'Schweigestill' an echo of Wahnfried, Wagner's last home in Bayreuth?) For the moment Leverkühn entertains no thought of settling at Schweigestill, and he and Schildknapp take themselves off to Italy for a couple of years, where work on the opera *Love's Labour's Lost* continues. It is during his stay in Italy that Leverkühn drafts his description of his encounter with the devil and of the pact which he then struck with him.

CHAPTER SIX

Dialogue with the Devil

We are in league and business—with your blood you have
affirmed it and promised yourself to us, and are baptized
ours. This my visit concerns only the confirmation there-
of. Time you have taken from us, a genius's time, high
flying time, full XXIV years *ab dato recessi*, which we set
to you as the limit. When they are finished and fully
expired, which is not to be foreseen, and such a time is
also an eternity—then you shall be fetched. Against this
meanwhile shall we be in all things subject and obedient,
and hell shall profit you, if you renay all living creature,
all the Heavenly Host and all men, for that must be.
(248)
Whosoever has built a 'new heaven' has found the
strength for it only in his own hell*.

The account of Leverkühn's meeting, dialogue, and pact
with the devil is one of the finest passages in *Doctor
Faustus*. Placed in the middle of the book, it is the apothe-
osis of what has gone before, and it sows the seeds of all
that is to follow. We shall be concerned in this chapter
not only with the psychology, morality and other aspects
(mainly negative) of Leverkühn's demonic pact, but also
to establish more generally the conditions under which
the extreme 'disobedience' implied by such pacts may
be justified, and may emerge as creative.

The dialogue with the devil takes place in 1911 or 1912
(Zeitblom is unable to assign the date with greater accur-
acy), during Leverkühn and Schildknapp's stay in Italy,

* Nietzsche, *On the Genealogy of Morals*, iii, 10.

at Palestrina, birthplace of the sixteenth-century composer.* The devil, in the guise of an insolent, red-haired scoundrel, 'with an actor's voice and eloquence' (224), appears to Leverkühn, who is alone in his room one evening with the shutters closed, recovering his strength after a severe attack of migraine: Schildknapp has gone down into the town for a drink and a game of billiards. The description of the meeting takes the form of a transcription by Zeitblom of Leverkühn's own record which, we are told, was made on music manuscript paper very shortly after the event and only came into Zeitblom's hands after the death of his friend.

This is a classic scene and Mann sounds the full resonance of a whole literary tradition of Faustian pacts and Mephistophelian dialogues.† Several important new

---

* Palestrina was a forerunner of Leverkühn's in that he, too, felt his gifts threatened by self-conscious intellectualism. Mann was also a fervent admirer of Hans Pfitzner's opera *Palestrina*, first given in Munich in June 1917 under Bruno Walter. Leverkühn's visit to Palestrina, the place, also has autobiographical reference, to which we shall return in a later chapter, for Mann himself stayed there in 1896–98 with his brother Heinrich—not with 'Schildknapp', who was modelled on the poet and translator Hans Reisiger who did not become Mann's friend until 1906.

† The affirmation of the pact, for example, is put into the devil's mouth in words which are virtually a direct quotation from the first Faust chapbook, the *Urfaustbuch* of 1587. These are the words which are placed at the head of the present chapter.

Mann's debt to Dostoevsky (which he freely acknowledges in *Genesis*) is also apparent here, as his devil dialogue is partly modelled on the famous passage describing Ivan Karamazov's encounter with the Grand Inquisitor. E. M. Butler has explored Mann's borrowing from Dostoevsky in her book *The Fortunes of Faust*. She points out that like Ivan, Adrian describes his visitor as a hateful and sordid person; he begins by doubting his reality, being half aware at first that it is a case of split personality; but, like Ivan, he is finally convinced of the contrary. Both are holding a monologue and mistake it for a dialogue; for both are trembling on the brink of madness. In both cases material objects (Ivan's handkerchief and glass of tea

twists are given to that tradition. The encounter with the devil is the direct result of the Faust concerned being clinically diseased, although, as we have seen, there is only the most superficial attempt to disguise the dialogue as anything other than psychological—the psyche in debate with itself. The positions taken up by the 'I' and the 'Thou' of the dialogue are not at all those of the usual run of Fausts and Mephistos; as Erich Heller has pointed out, it is now Mephisto who supplies the soul, Faust the indifferent omnicompetence. * Furthermore, everything is reasoned; it is a long, painful argument. The two roles, Heller observes, are an exact inversion of those in Goethe's version of the legend, and Mann's is a book of Faust's damnation rather than of his eventual redemption. I shall return to this theme in my last chapter when considering the place of Mann's musical Faust within the post sixteenth-century Faust tradition as a whole. For our present orientation it is sufficient to relate Mann's version to Goethe's.

Goethe's Faust acknowledges an essential unity between himself and the world; for him salvation lies in refusing transcendence and placing complete trust in the power of his own faculties, faculties which, he believes, 'can comprehend/The Wondrous Architecture of the World' (Marlowe). His Mephisto is the embodiment of critique, irony and mockery, who would break Faust's faith and enthusiasm and trick him into damning, easeful contentment. The price for Faust's place in heaven is eternal striving and rejection of the Mephistophelian

---

and Adrian's coat and rug) prove that there was no reality in the apparition; but both men are too far gone in delusion by then to believe the testimony of their own eyes.

* HIG, 267–8, and see also Erich Heller's essay 'Faust's Damnation' in HAJ, especially pp. 37–44.

option. By contrast, Mann's Faustus is an aristocratic nihilist whose faculties find themselves deeply at odds with the architecture of the world. Leverkühn is 'condemned to the sphere of higher parody, the only thing that is still left when the "real thing" has become impossible, and the "direct method" of creation, as the Devil has it, "incompatible with genuineness" ' (HIG, 267). For this Faust, redemption and ultimate salvation are only to be won by invocation of the devil, who offers 'shining, sparkling, vainglorious unreflectiveness' (237) to revalidate the 'direct method' and restore some measure of faith in reality and in the realities revealed through art.

Both Leverkühn's pact and dialogue are, like all such pacts and dialogues, not with the supposed devil, but with the self. An important implication of these dialogues is a rejection of the possibility of dialogue with any reality (particularly of transcendent aspect) other than that of one's own person.* Leverkühn's pact is also much more dangerous and uncertain than the guaranteed bargains that Fausts of yore had been able to strike with their respective Mephistos. The promises made by Leverkühn's demon are the wild hopes of the diseased experimenter, voiced in an unreal, archaic German designed to reinforce the unreality with which he wishes to identify himself.

*   *   *

* Such quests for latent existential possibilities lay those undertaking them wide open to self deception for (as Jung has observed) preoccupation with the demonic aspects of one's psychopathology may be an escape from 'unacceptable' reality (JSM, 91–3). The introspective vision tends to lose its primordial quality and become merely a symptom, instead of a portal giving on to a maturer, reintegrated psyche.

In a brief introduction to his transcription, Zeitblom wastes little time in wondering whether it is the record of an actual or imaginary dialogue:

> A dialogue? Is it really a dialogue? I should be mad to believe it. And therefore I cannot believe that in the depths of his soul Adrian himself considered to be actual that which he saw and heard—either while he heard and saw it or afterwards, when he put it on paper; notwithstanding the cynicism with which his interlocutor sought to convince him of his objective presence. (221)

The appearance of the devil and Leverkühn's consequent dialogue with him is provoked by the musician reading Kierkegaard, specifically a passage about Mozart's *Don Giovanni*.* An apposite text certainly, for it was perhaps not so much the Don's audacity and impertinence, as his disbelief and defiance of the dark forces, which stung the stone guest to a practical demonstration of their reality. Leverkühn's guest, who brings with him into the room an icy, freezing draught, comments specifically on the composer's reading matter:

> If I mistake not, you were reading just now in a book by the Christian in love with aesthetics. He knew and understood my particular relation to this beautiful art— (the most Christian of all arts, he finds—but Christian in reverse, as it were: introduced and developed by Christianity indeed, but then rejected and banned as the Devil's Kingdom—so there you are). A highly theological business, music—the way sin is, the way I am. The passion of that Christian for music is true passion, and as such knowledge and corruption in one. For there is true passion only in the ambiguous and ironic. The highest passion concerns the absolutely questionable. (242)

* Kierkegaard's notion that genius was *ipso facto* sinful has exercised a great influence on German thought and, not least, on Thomas Mann: see E. M. Butler, *The Fortunes of Faust*, p. 327.

The debate swiftly passes to that ambiguity between appearance and reality which was discussed in the previous chapter *à propos* the scientific experiments of Leverkühn's father Jonathan. This leitmotif now re-appears:

> I: ' . . . I am to grow osmotic growths.'
> He: 'It comes to the same thing. Ice crystals, or the same made of starch, sugar, and cellulose, both are nature; we ask, for which shall we praise Nature more . . .'
> (242)

This idea is suggestively linked to the question of the subjective or objective reality of the devil's visit—the plain implication being that it *is* subjective:

> Your tendency, my friend, to inquire after the objective, the so-called truth, to question as worthless the subjective, pure experience: that is truly petty bourgeois, you ought to overcome it [says the devil]. As you see me, so I exist to you.   (242)

*   *   *

As we have seen, the syphilitic infection which liberated the powers of Leverkühn's unconscious and promoted their domination of his rational faculties, had been quite deliberately sought out by him. The dialogue may be read as an elaborate *post facto* explanation and inquisition of the decision taken between the first and second meetings with Hetaera Esmeralda, cast in the form of a debate between the rational and irrational powers, with the latter eventually winning the upper hand. Mann shows successively in Leverkühn the sterilities of extreme reason and unreason, the syphilitic infection serving as the onset of the transition from the one to the other. We see first of all an excess of cold knowledge, intellect and reason, unwarmed by feeling or any other kind of instinctive impulse. Once the infection is caught, Leverkühn draws more and more on free unconscious impulse, accepting as disciplinary censor an arbitrary intellectual system (that of the 12-tone Method) itself, which for Mann is simply one more cunning property from the cupboard of the magical and irrational.

Leverkühn's first unintentional visit to the Leipzig brothel awakens him for the first time to the raw possibilities of the instinctual forces. Feeling that the pressure of rational thought on the free exercise of instinct and imagination has grown intolerable, he is suddenly aware of the zymotic possibility of its permanent relief. Thus it is with his eyes newly opened that he seeks out his poisonous butterfly. The dialogue itself confirms the deliberation behind the second encounter with the black-eyed girl.

The devil insists that he is 'no unbidden guest' and describes himself as 'Esmeralda's friend and cohabitant'. 'Do you still remember?' counters the devil to Leverkühn's insistence that his guest was uninvited: 'The philosopher [Aristotle], *De anima*: "the acts of the person acting are performed on him the previously disposed to suffer it". There you have it: on the disposition, the readiness, the invitation, all depends' (233). The devil's reference is to that unaccountable anticipation which is so often a prerequisite for finding new experience meaningful. Writing of Schopenhauer's influence on Wagner, Ernest Newman quotes Pascal's view of all similar phenomena of apparently sudden spiritual revelation and re-birth: ' "You would not have sought me unless you had already found me" ' Thus it had been with Wagner: 'Schopenhauer merely reinforced his emotions and intuitions with reasons and arguments';* thus too it

* *The Life of Richard Wagner*, op. cit., Vol. 2, p. 431.

was to be with Leverkühn, the exterior 'traumatic' event crystallizing and bringing to a head the already present tendency, just as the quaffing of the love potion in the first act of *Tristan* serves principally to bring to consciousness that which is already fully prepared in the unconscious.

We learn from the devil that the doctors whom Leverkühn sought out to treat his infection were put away in his interest, indeed that their efforts to cure the general infiltration had but 'given a powerful impetus to the metastasis upwards, their business was accomplished, they had to be removed. The fools, to wit, do not know, and if they know they cannot change it, that by the general treatment the upper, the meta-venereal processes are powerfully accelerated' (234). For his part, Leverkühn had fought down his remaining doubts and scruples when be abandoned his frustrated search for a cure.

It is in this conscious seeking out of the 'blind inspired state' that Leverkühn's attributed immorality, his disobedience, may be seen most clearly to lie. On the theme of the necessity, and higher morality, of immorality and disobedience, there will be more to say. For the present we notice that the devil offers Leverkühn inspiration, unparalysed by thought or by the mortal domination of reason:

> We make naught new [promises the devil]–that is other people's matter. We only release, only set free. We let the lameness and self-consciousness, the chaste scruples and doubts go to the Devil. . . . A genuine inspiration, immediate, absolute, unquestioned, ravishing, where there is no choice, no tinkering, no possible improvement; . . . no, that is not possible with God, who leaves the understanding too much to do. It comes but from the devil, the true master and giver of such rapture. (236–7)

The devil holds up to Leverkühn the example of Beethoven and his work processes as revealed in his notebooks. There the 'idea' is but the raw material, the signal for the start of the real work. In the notebooks, 'there is no thematic conception there as God gave it. He [Beethoven] remoulds it and adds "Meilleur." Scant confidence in God's prompting, scant respect for it is expressed in that "Meilleur"—itself not so very enthusiastic either' (237).

*　　　*　　　*

The psychology of the release Mann had in mind here may best be understood in the light of his response to Freud, and to Schopenhauer whom he considered to have anticipated Freud. Schopenhauer's assertion of the primacy of instinct over mind and reason had made on the young Mann what he was to describe later as a 'shattering impression'. He soon discovered that this philosophy was supported by the psychology of Freud, with which it shared a common moral attitude:

> Freud's description of the id and the ego—is it not to a hair Schopenhauer's description of the Will and the Intellect, a translation of the latter's metaphysics into psychology? So he who had been initiated into the metaphysics of Schopenhauer, and in Nietzsche tasted the painful pleasure of psychology—he must needs have been filled with a sense of recognition and familiarity when first, encouraged thereto by its denizens, he entered the realms of psychoanalysis and looked about him. . . . (E3D, 417)

The pact Leverkühn strikes with what we may describe as 'the devil of his unconscious life' is the prelude to a trial of the artistic potential of the id after the powers of mind, reason and metaphysic have been rejected. It is a

G

trial of whatever laws are to be found within, when
extreme self-consciousness of language and self forbid the
acceptance of objective guiding principles from without.
It is an attempted renunciation of the *plus royal que le
roi* Faustian sin of knowledge before which innocence
and imagination have been forced to retreat. Its purpose,
like that of the Expressionists, is to deny 'objective reality' by diving below appearance and consciousness to
tap the spontaneous irrational energies previously unknown, forbidden, or otherwise unavailable. A classic
instance is Schoenberg's monodrama *Erwartung* (Expect-
ation) of 1909, composed in a creative frenzy of seventeen
days. The text—a mere sketch which allows the music
to mirror the turbulence of the unconscious life—is significantly by Marie Pappenheim, one of the early psycho-
analysts. In his essay 'Freud and the Future' (in E3D),
Mann refers directly to the readiness with which the id,
that 'melting pot of seething excitations', lends itself to
exploitation. It is, he says, 'not organized, produces no
collective will, merely the striving to achieve satisfaction
for the impulsive needs operating under the pleasure
principle'. There can be no doubt whom he has in mind
when he goes on to speak of the moral devastation of a
whole mass-ego 'which is produced by worship of the
unconscious, the glorification of its dynamic as the only
life-promoting force, the systematic glorification of the
primitive and irrational'. For the id, he stresses, knows no
values, is beyond good and evil and has no morality.
Leverkühn's sacrifice to the Dionysian unconscious is
thus to be taken as downright immoral and power-
seeking in the sense in which Nietzsche would have
acknowledged these words.

The conflict in *Fiorenza*, Mann's early play of 1904,
between those two great wounded men of power, Savon-

arola and Lorenzo de Medici—the sacred and secular
sides to the same coin—is vividly recalled:

> THE PRIOR [Savonarola]: . . . an inward fire burns in
> my limbs and urges me to the pulpit.
> LORENZO: An inward fire—I know. I know! I know this
> fire, I have called it daemon, will, frenzy—but it has
> no name. It is the madness of him who offers himself
> up to an unknown god . . .   (SOL1, 315)

Mann made no bones about attributing the hateful madness of Hitler to a monstrous miscarriage of the artistic
impulse: 'I quietly suspect', he wrote in his 1938 essay
'Brother Hitler',

> that the frenzy which drove him into a certain capital
> [Vienna] was aimed at the old analyst who lived there,
> his true and most personal enemy, the philosophical man
> Freud who has revealed the nature of neurosis, and
> administers sobriety and sobering knowledge even about
> 'genius'. *

To the Freudian, furthermore, there is a close association
between the concepts of evil and culture which gives
added point to Mann's projection of political evils on to
the person of Leverkühn, the composer.

*   *   *

And thus Mann himself would administer sobering
knowledge about the power of the wounded psyche. Like
the id itself this power is dangerous because of its inherent
instability; it asks no questions about the ends to which
it may be deployed. The moral responsibility rests with
the Faust who would draw on it, and he himself, as Jung
has suggested, is generally—and Leverkühn is no exception—an ambivalent figure embodying not only

> the archetype of the Wise Old Man, the helper and
> redeemer, but also of the magician, deceiver, corruptor

* Quoted in HIG, 91.

and tempter. This image has lain buried and dormant in
the unconscious since the dawn of history: it is awakened
whenever the times are out of joint and a great error
deflects society from the right path. (JSM, 103)

Jung goes on to assert that

> the seductive error is like a poison that can also act as a
> cure, and the shadow of a saviour can turn into a fiendish
> destroyer. These opposing forces are at work in the
> mythical healer himself: the physician who heals wounds
> is himself the bearer of a wound . . .*

The conditions under which the poison may be able to
act as a cure will be considered shortly. For the moment
it is important to emphasize Mann's critical concern
with that miscarriage of the artistic impulse whose consequences are totally evil and opposed to human values.
What is involved here is not a down-to-earth matter of
good and evil, but rather one of a supermorality 'beyond
good and evil' and outside the confines of all rigid,
authoritarian orthodoxies and systems of morality.

The blacker aspects of Nietzsche's thought come to
the fore, when the devil assures Leverkühn that:

> . . . an untruth of a kind that enhances power holds its
> own against any ineffectively virtuous truth. . . . I have

---

* This raises an interesting point which helps to explain one of
Leverkühn's exceptional Faustian characteristics, his moral standing.
Jung stresses that Fausts are usually unwounded and that this means
that they are untouched by the moral problem. 'A man can be as
high-minded as Faust and as devilish as Mephistopheles if he is able
to split his personality into two halves, and only then is he capable
of feeling "six thousand feet beyond good and evil". ' But, as we have
seen, Mann's Leverkühn *is* wounded—his syphilis being the physical
symbol of the wound —and this is a clear affirmation of his excessive moral obsession. '. . . She told me herself that she had no
morality—', Nietzsche wrote of Lou Andreas-Salomé to Paul Rée
in 1882, 'and I thought she had, like myself, a more severe
morality than anybody . . .'. (NK, 102)

never heard anything stupider then [sic] that from disease only disease can come. Life is not scrupulous—by
morals it sets not a fart. It takes the reckless product of
disease, feeds on and digests it, and as soon as it takes it
to itself it is health. Before the fact of fitness for life, my
good man, all distinction of disease and health falls
away. (242)

The immediate continuation of this passage is a direct
indictment of the Third Reich and of those who exalted
it, often in the belief that it was divinely ordained:

A whole host and generation of youth, receptive, sound
to the core, flings itself on the work of the morbid genius,
made genius by disease: admires it, praises it, exalts it,
carries it away, assimilates it unto itself and makes it over
to culture, which lives not on home-made bread alone,
but as well on provender and poison from the apothecary's
shop at the sign of the Blessed Messengers. (242–3)

Thus aberration is built on aberration and the whole
becomes self-sanctifying. 'On your madness they will
feed in health, and in them you will become healthy',
the devil tells Leverkühn. But far from the one aberration
setting the situation to rights, in the political and ethical
sphere (as distinct from the artistic) it fathers a whole
host of even more malignant offspring.

*   *   *

The theme of the artist's special insights flourishing
in protest against, or in compensation for some deep and
incurable wound, is familiar, but it is one of which Mann
never tired and in the service of whose re-statement he
was always prepared to be more or less frankly autobiographical. The confessional passages in *Faustas* have only
to be set against earlier ones, particularly those in *Tonio
Kröger* (1903) written more than forty years previously,
to show that although his political ideas changed very

considerably, his personal artistic credo remained firm.*
He believed that artistic effort was not a re-enactment of
the first Creation, something essentially 'good', but rather
something 'bad', an aberration inviting psychological
enquiry. Those who are touched by his art would, Tonio
Kröger feels, 'freeze up if they were to get a look behind
the scenes. What they, in their innocence, cannot comprehend is that a properly constituted, healthy, decent
man never writes, acts or composes . . .'. The artistic
'gift', 'rests upon extremely sinister foundations' (SOL1,
177). Throughout his life Mann subscribed to this
Nietzschean notion, although his attitude to psychological knowledge became less confident as time went by.
Difficulties are already apparent in Nietzsche's own
exposition in *Beyond Good and Evil:*

> Those great poets, for example, men like Byron, Musset,
> Poe, Leopardi, Kleist, Gogol–I do not dare mention far
> greater names, but I mean them– . . . all with souls in
> which they must usually conceal some fracture; often
> taking revenge with their works for some inner con-
> tamination, often seeking in their lofty flights escape into
> forgetfulness from an all-too-faithful memory; idealists
> from the vicinity of *swamps*–what a torture are these
> great artists and all the so-called higher men to him who
> has guessed their true nature!   (NK, 678–9)

Having got thus far Nietzsche found himself compelled,
with imperfect consistency, to conclude that 'it follows
that it is the mark of a finer humanity to respect "the
mask" and not, in the wrong places, indulge in psychology

---

* His very awareness of the credo proclaims him for the highly
sophisticated *sentimentalisch* (in Schiller's sense), or alienated, writer
that he was–yet the constancy of that credo is, curiously, something
more often associated with the *naiv* artist, i.e., in the opposed
category in Schiller's distinction. The *naiv* artist would not consider
there to be any discontinuity between himself and the flux of the
people and world around him.

and curiosity', thus saddling writer and reader alike with
a vexing dilemma. For, recognizing with Nietzsche that
the questioner bears a moral responsibility for the values
implicit in the answers he seeks, one is caught between
tearing away the mask by turning psychologist, or
respecting it and trying to come to terms with the uncomfortable idea that the good and beautiful may often be
fleurs du mal. The first alternative ultimately devalues
all art save that of the psychologist himself.

Erich Heller attributes the 'failure' (judged by the
most severe criteria) of Mann's early play *Fiorenza* to the
writer's psychological approach, which, he says, is so representative of our age. 'This psychology', writes Heller,

> cannot but render meaningless the great gestures of the
> human spirit. For it contemplates them in a spiritual
> vacuum. Yet at the same time the writer is engaged in
> the paradoxical business of extracting from it aesthetic
> significance: a work of literature. And *Fiorenza*, in its
> dealing with men of power and religion is, of course,
> particularly engendered by this paradox.   (HIG, 92)

But twelve years later, and twenty before the essay on
Freud, Mann was to denounce psychology as 'the cheapest
and meanest' manner of knowing because there is 'nothing
on earth, no belief, no feeling, no passion, which could
not be reduced to worthlessness by psychological analysis'.* Mann could have gone further here, for those who
honour the mask bear an obvious and essential responsibility: to guard against their vulnerability to all manner
of emotional coercion and indecent persuasion through
the irrational. It is certainly in this light that Mann's
political indictment of the rise of the Third Reich and
the inadequate resistance to it should be seen.

Freud shared Nietzsche's and Mann's belief that the

* Quoted in HIG, 93.

artistic 'gift' rests upon 'extremely sinister foundations', but he was no respecter of masks, and systematically set out to penetrate them. The psychologist held that anyone who questioned the meaning of life was ill, thus neatly dismissing the question of 'meaning'. But he did not intend to skate over difficulties such as this quite so lightly and, as Dr Charles Rycroft has suggested, what he must have meant by this was that 'living itself gives meaning to life and that this is doubted only by those who have become to some measure self-alienated, and who as a result have recourse to religious or ideological theories of meaning as a "secondary construction", an attempt to restore the lost sense of meaningfulness by deriving it from some source external to the self'.* To this should perhaps be added the 'secondary worlds' created through art. By Freud's criteria, anyone like Leverkühn who looks for 'meaning' deep down in the self and in the self alone is nothing if not chronically 'ill'. Psychology, though, is scarcely equipped to assess the worth of any 'meaning', artistic or otherwise, that may —at a price which few would wish to be called on to pay— be found there. This price, which Leverkühn pays, is the renunciation of the love generally considered to furnish the best available meaning of our humanity. This love is to be contrasted with that cold love, either of self or of religious or ideological 'secondary constructions',† which is inhuman and anti-human in that it will readily sacrifice the primacy of inter-personal relationships to that of the unreciprocable relationship between an individual and some absolute external or internal authority.

* *Psychoanalysis Observed*, Penguin edition, Harmondsworth, 1968, p. 20.

† The 'secondary constructions' of the artist are either inhumanly personal and private, or loving celebrations of the best of a shared humanity.

'Cold we want you to be, that the fires of creation shall be hot enough to warm yourself in', says the devil. 'Into them you will flee out of the cold of your life . . .' (249). Leverkühn resists this strongly and uncomprehendingly for, he protests, had he not inaugurated the whole business through a variety of this very love: ' . . . what is then the course of it, prithee, but love, even if that poisoned by you with God's sanction? The bond in which you assert we stand has itself to do with love, you doating fool.' The devil is not so lightly deceived, as even he is not prepared to recognize *this* variety as love. So he qualifies his terms and points out that by love he means that which is humanly warm, for it is only *that* which arouses 'the legitimate jealousy of hell'.

Leverkühn is eventually won to the proposition when he has convinced himself that it is merely the acknowledgement and confirmation of a tendency already present: 'A general chilling of your life and your relations to men lies in the nature of things—rather it lies already in your nature'; the devil points out, 'in feith we lay upon you nothing new, the little ones make nothing new and strange out of you, they only ingeniously strengthen and exaggerate all that you already are.' Leverkühn vainly objects that it would seem to be 'hell in advance, which is already offered me on earth', but it is his devil who is left with the last word in the shape of a presumptive question, 'Do you strike with me?'—meaning that the pact is sealed. The apparition vanishes and Leverkühn discovers Schildknapp, back from town, sitting in the sofa-corner in his place.

*   *   *

Ascetic renunciation of physical and emotional affections has always been relied on for strengthening 'the

vehemence and inwardliness of the religious instinct'.*
Such renunciation also intensifies that dangerous state
of 'a passion for truth, but no belief in it' and this takes
us back to the conversation, quoted in the previous chapter, when Zeitblom asks Leverkühn whether he knows
a stronger emotion than love.

> 'Yes,' Leverkühn replies, 'interest.'
> 'By which you presumably mean a love from which the
> animal warmth has been withdrawn.'
> 'Let us agree on the definition!' he laughed.

In deciding what they want out of life, people have
always had to choose between the equation of love and
death (as celebrated in Wagner's *Tristan*) and that of
love and life (I am, because I love): this latter equation
being the foundation on which post-Renaissance humanism was built. Once the former equation has been
affirmed, two alternatives present themselves—either to
return to life in love, or to press forward, forswearing
love with an intensity equal to that with which one
would embrace whatever is still allowable and available
of life, only life in its anti-human, dehumanized aspect.
This last variety partakes of a grim immortality, reminiscent of the horror of Nietzsche's idea of eternal recurrence. This, surely, is the state of which the closing
words of Father Zosima's final discourse in *The Brothers
Karamazov* are intended to remind the reader: he talks
of those

> fearful ones who have given themselves over to Satan and
> his proud spirit entirely. For such, hell is voluntary and
> ever consuming; they are tortured by their own choice.
> For they have cursed themselves, cursing God and life.
> . . . they cry out that the God of life should be annihil-

* The phrase is Nietzsche's: NK, 591.

ated, that God should destroy Himself and His own
creation. And they will burn in the fire of their own
wrath and for ever yearn for death and annihilation. But
they will not attain to death . . .*

This same discourse begins with Father Zosima ponder-
ing 'What is hell?' and suggesting that it is the suffering
of being unable to love. 'Once in infinite existence, im-
measurable in time and space, a spiritual creature was
given on his coming to earth, the power of saying, "I am
and I love".' It is the fate of Leverkühn (and all who,
like him, reject this invitation to life) which Father
Zosima has in mind when he speculates that 'if there
were fire in material agony, their still greater spiritual
agony cannot be taken from them, for that suffering is
not external but within them'.

*   *   *

The long history of Faustian literature makes it clear
that an essential ingredient of devilish pacts is the renunciation of love—even where this is not immediately
apparent. After Gretchen, various manifestations of 'the
eternal Feminine', including Marie Godeau, proclaim
the lie of the 'leads us on high'—for him who has for-
sworn love there can be no redemption, even by love.
The quest for omnipotence, for man to become as a God,
has however always proved so supremely attractive that
there has been no shortage of those eager to renounce
love for its sake. The example of Alberich would have
left an indelible impression on Mann's mind. It is Alberich's theft of the gold which violates the unchanging
harmony of the Ring's *Urwelt* and sets the tremendous
dramatic cycle into rotation; it is the first and greatest
of a whole series of pivotal crimes which determine the

* Dostoevsky, *The Brothers Karamazov*, Everyman edition,
London, 1957, Vol. 1, p. 336.

progress of the drama. 'Only he who forswears love's power', Woglinde reassures her Rhine-sisters, 'only he who banishes love's delight, only he attains the magic to forge a ring from the gold.'* Reassures, because how could their gold be in danger from a lecherous dwarf whose insatiable greed for what would scarcely pass as love was the reason for his visit to the three sisters? Perhaps it is their vanity that leads them to overestimate the importance of 'love' to their adversary, for Alberich, when he knows what is required, tears the gold from the rock: 'I put out your light; snatch the gold from the rock; forge the ring of revenge; for, let the waters hear it! so I curse love.'*

Such an act, as we have noted, has a light as well as a dark side to it, and Wagner immediately draws our attention to the light side in the music. As Robert Donington so well describes it, if Alberich's deed were finally and irredeemably blasphemous

> 'with nothing else implied, the music conveying it would have to be inexpressibly dreary, empty and at the same time, final. It is nothing of the kind. It is full of significance, baleful indeed, but strangely moving, questing, and above all suggesting not an end but a beginning, which is exactly what it is. It is almost as if the music were urging us to ask: can good come out of this terrible deed?'†

Leverkühn, too, commits this scandalous disobedience of forswearing love and we must now look at the conditions and occasions under which such disobedience may emerge as creative.

*   *   *

* *Das Rheingold*, libretto translated into English by William Mann, The Friends of Covent Garden, London, 1964, p. 26–8.

† Robert Donington, *Wagner's 'Ring' and its Symbols*, Faber and Faber, London, 1963, p. 64.

The artist's *proper* disobedience has its motive in his necessity to do something new: nothing must prevent him asserting his own ideas, and hence he will break the old law wherever it offends. His manifesto takes the form, 'No, no, you are wrong, it is not thus, but *thus!*' This is what Dostoevsky's Raskolnikoff means when he speaks of a superior class who strive to break the law— 'Most of these insist upon destruction of what exists in the name of what ought to exist.' Raskolnikoff's insistence on the necessary disobedience of the *Übermensch* marks him out as one of Leverkühn's precursors. Readers of Dostoevsky will recall how Raskolnikoff, this student of the law, writes an article setting forth the view

> that Nature divided men into two categories: the first, an inferior one, comprising ordinary men, the kind of material whose function it is to reproduce specimens like themselves; the other, a superior one, comprising men who have the gift or power to make a new word, thought, or deed felt . . .

This second category consisted

> exclusively of men who break the law, or strive, according to their capacity or power to do so. . . .Most of these insist upon destruction of what exists in the name of what ought to exist. And if, in the execution of their idea, they should be obliged to shed blood, step over corpses, they can conscientiously do both in the interest of their idea, not otherwise—pray mark this. *

Raskolnikoff's ideas, in common with those of many of Dostoevsky's characters, demand that we consider the limits to which the means may be stretched. It is all very well for Nietzsche to tell us that 'whoever must be a creator in good and evil, verily, he must first be an

* *Crime and Punishment*, Everyman edition, London, 1933, p. 194.

annihilator and break values. Thus the highest evil belongs to the highest goodness: but this is creative' (NK, 228). Or for Goethe's Mephistopheles to describe himself as 'part of a power that would alone work evil, but engenders good'.* Just how far should or can one go? For the hazard is complete absorption into evil. It is the perennial problem of effectively opposing evil without being affected or caught up in it, a problem which assumes alarming proportions should evil deliberately be employed against evil. The dialogue with the devil shows Leverkühn putting up an appreciable resistance to the evil which offers itself to him, but that resistance is insufficient. As he cannot himself subject the evil, he must be subject to it.

Leverkühn's disobedience is in fact doubly disobedient in that it is not in the name of science and reason, but in that of unreason, or amoral instinctive fertility and power. This disobedience is not least provoked by an excess of scientific rationalist pressure upon that perfectly reasonable metaphysical breathing space which Nietzsche demanded: 'all the highest questions, all the highest value problems, lie beyond human reason. To comprehend the limits of reason—that alone is truly philosophy' (NK, 641). Nietzsche reminds us that Kant had considered philosophy's task as being 'to open the way again for faith by showing knowledge its limits' (NK, 85). And Nietzsche is not here as inconsistent as he might seem, for what he hated was neither faith nor reason (he wanted the highest, most intense forms of both), but their tendencies towards dogma and system which stifled the spirit of free, open enquiry and also that of spontaneous, Dionysian creative exuberance. 'I mis-

* *Faust*, Part One, translated by Philip Wayne, Penguin, Harmondsworth, 1949, p. 75.

trust all systematizers and I avoid them,' he wrote. 'The will to a system is a lack of integrity' (NK, 470). Thus the creatively disobedient Leverkühn, the disciple of Nietzsche, falls short of the philosopher's teaching when he discovers, and is duly exploited by, a rigorous musical system of his own.

We may now try to summarize the respective positive and negative aspects of Leverkühn's disobedience. The negative aspects are dominant (being for the most part thinly disguised political and psychological criticism and commentary on the susceptibilities of the German psyche), while the positive aspects are associated most closely with the cultural tradition, especially in its musical aspect.

Leverkühn's artistic disobedience is motivated by apparently insoluble difficulties inherent in the musical tradition, the extreme exhaustion of which required an extreme deed for it to enjoy a further lease of life. His technical disobedience—the overthrow of classical tonality, negation of the natural relationships of the notes within it, and the imposition of a new 'principle capable of serving as a rule'—are all legitimate in that they serve an altogether new expressive intention unrealizable by the vocabulary and syntax which he inherited. The disobedience here incurred is artistically necessary, for the communication of new meaning resides to a very large extent in the crossing of expectations derived from our experience of the language and its usage to date. And this linguistic revolution, although it may pass through a phase of anarchy (cf., the 'free atonality' of Schoenberg's more extreme expressionist compositions), is acceptable because it establishes limits, limits at least as strict as any established before. As Leverkühn tells Zeitblom, in adopting the 12-tone Method the composer would be 'bound by a self-imposed compulsion to order, hence free' (193).

In its negative aspect, Leverkühn's disobedience is culpable principally because of his taking absolute and irreversible measures in the service of an unlimited revolutionary goal. These measures include the acceptance of limits but, because of their intractability, they are disqualified as such. To be truly creative and morally acceptable, formal constraints in any field should be in process of continual self-evaluation and change.

Further, as Albert Camus, who has movingly discussed the light and dark sides to disobedience in *L'homme révolté*, has shown, the limits of the good rebellion (which may be seen in its pure state in artistic creation) are those 'where minds meet, and in meeting begin to exist'. The common ground is that on which every man bases his first values, and Camus therefore coined the famous slogan, 'I *rebel*—therefore we *exist*'. Thus the good rebel is prepared to sacrifice himself for the common good—as perhaps Nietzsche may have tried to do. But Leverkühn's disobedience, especially in so far as this is associated with German nationalism, is of its essence personal—it is a deliberate plunge away from contact with others down into the depths of his own being. The hermetic totalitarianism of such a path leads almost inevitably to an eventual desire for an apocalypse, and Leverkühn's penultimate composition, the *Apocalypsis cum figuris* based on Dürer's woodcut series, celebrates just this desire.

Leverkühn's major disobedience, his deliberate second visit to the infected whore, is an act of indeterminate consequence. It is a violation of normal physiology with unpredictable pathological result. The gamble is considered worth making in the hope of winning a cultural

breakthrough—but to what? No goal is declared at this
stage in terms other than those of unlimited revolution:
'We only release, only set free', says the devil. 'What he
wants and gives . . . is shining, sparkling, vainglorious
unreflectiveness! . . . a sacred mandate, a visitation
received by the possessed one with faltering and stumb-
ling step . . .' (236-7).

The good rebellion, says Camus, asks whether a rule of
conduct may be found outside religion and outside any
system of absolute values. But Leverkühn's rebellion is
rootedly religious and absolute. Artistic activity, musical
composition, is for him the highest form of theological
speculation. It is for this that he deserts academic theological studies, and his major disobedience is marked by
the 'leap of faith' characteristic of the religious. His
principle of musical organization becomes the natural
expression of an absolute confidence in the irrational.

CHAPTER SEVEN

The Apocalyptic Oratorio

Leverkühn and Schildknapp return from Palestrina to Munich in the autumn of 1912. Before the end of October the composer has taken up residence as lodger at the same Schweigstill farmhouse at Pfeiffering, * which he had previously singled out as a possible permanent home while on the bicycling expedition with Schild-knapp. There he settles down to his work, seldom to be interrupted either by visitors or by his own excursions. Isolationist by temperament, he has no desire to attend performances of his music–a preference from which not even the clever Jewish impresario Saul Fitelberg (another demonic figure) is able to dissuade him.

The following year (1913) Zeitblom secures a teaching post at Freising† where he settles with his wife and child –in reach both of Pfeiffering and of Munich, whose salons are the setting for most of the novel's social content. Zeitblom's story finds its material in Leverkühn's compositions, in the speculative discussions on art, cultural history and politics which take place on the rare occasions when Leverkühn has company, and in the Munich intellectual milieu into which the composer is drawn from time to time. The opera *Love's Labour's Lost* is duly completed (and given, unsuccessfully, in Lübeck) and there follow the Blake songs, previously mentioned, settings of

* In reality, Polling, thirty miles south-west of Munich.
† Twenty miles north-east of Munich.

Keats (the 'Ode to a Nightingale' and the 'Ode to Melancholy'), and a full-scale work for baritone, organ, and
string orchestra, based on Klopstock's *Spring Festival*.
This last, Zeitblom understands, is a 'plea to God, an
atonement for sin, a work of *attritio cordis*, composed as
I realized with shudders, under the threat of that visitor
insisting that he was really visible' (266). The piece is
given its first performance during the First World War
and is repeated later in several German music-centres
and also in Switzerland. By the early 1920s Leverkühn's
music is making its way, and 'an aura of esoteric fame
began to unfold about the name of my friend' (265). In
the last months of 1913 and the first of 1914, Leverkühn
writes an orchestral fantasy *Marvels of the Universe*
which, says Zeitblom, 'has contributed not a little to the
reproach levelled at the art of my friend, as an antiartistic virtuosity, a blasphemy, a nihilistic sacrilege'
(275).

When the War breaks out Zeitblom joins up, but not
Leverkühn nor any others from their circle: 'In nearly
all the men of our group there turned out to be some kind
of weakness, something we had scarcely known, but it
now procured their exemption' (302). An apocalyptic note
is struck in the description of the 1914 Munich carnival,
those last days of an epoch 'which put an end for ever
to the idyll of aesthetic guilelessness in the city on the
Isar' (285).

Leverkühn's next work is a *Gesta Romanorum* suite
(1914–15) for the puppet theatre, with speaker, voices,
and a small orchestra of violin, double-bass, clarinet, bassoon, trumpet, trombone and percussion. This is based
on texts from the famous collection of romantic myths of
the Middle Ages known by that name * and in it Lever-

* Mann's source was the third edition of the *Gesta Romanorum*,

kühn tilts at decadent romanticism by adopting a drily neoclassical style and by indulging his penchant for parody. He treats his fantastic and frequently scandalous subject matter as further evidence for the tragi-comic jesting of the Creator – as manifestations comparable with the scientific phenomena which so moved his father Jonathan, but to him were but a source of unholy mirth.

Both the musical and theatrical aspects of the *Gesta Romanorum* are of interest in that the chamber instrumentation, the placing of the singers in the pit and the reliance on a speaker who unfolds the story in a narrative and recitative, are unusual features which might well have been modelled on Stravinsky's anti-romantic theatre pieces, *Reynard* (1916) and *The Soldier's Tale* (1918). These two works are the embodiment of parodistic critique of the romantic art epoch. We do not know whether these really are the models for this particular musical fiction, but the correspondence is almost as exact as that between Leverkühn's late String Trio (1927) and Schoenberg's Op. 45 (1946) on which it was deliberately modelled. Leverkühn's Muse acknowledges no traditional territorial demarcation.

These and the other works, however, are completely overshadowed by the two principal compositions of Leverkühn's maturity, namely the *Apocalypsis cum figuris* (completed in 1919) and the *Lamentation of Dr. Faustus* which dates from 1929 and 1930, the last two years of his creative life – his devil's time. It is with these 'two

---

das älteste Mährchen und Legendenbuch des christlischen Mittelalters, edited by J. T. Grasse, Leipzig, 1905. Mann makes more or less verbatim use of Dr Grasse's German translations from the Latin. One of Leverkühn's chosen texts, 'On the Birth of the Holy Pope Gregory' was later expanded by Mann himself into his novel *The Holy Sinner* (1951).

chief monuments of his proud and austere life' (453) that this chapter and the next will be concerned.

Mann's gift for evoking music in words is nowhere more apparent than in Zeitblom's descriptions of Leverkühn's two masterworks. These evocations are the more remarkable in that the 'music' would seem to have been largely a product of the writer's imagination. The *Apocalypsis* is a cantata inspired by Dürer's set of fifteen woodcuts of the same title. It is, says Zeitblom, its composer's most representative work,

> a journey into hell, wherein are worked through the visional representations of the hereafter, (in the earlier, shamanistic stages, as well as those developed from antiquity and Christianity, down to Dante). (358)

The *Apocalypsis* is an expressionist trial of the powers of darkness, reminiscent in some respects of a work to which reference has already been made in another context (p. 49), Schoenberg's oratorio *Die Jakobsleiter* (1917–22, but unfinished), a transitional piece poised between the atonal expressionism of *Erwartung* and the new classicism defined by the first strict-style 12-tone compositions. *Die Jakobsleiter* was originally conceived as the fourth movement of an unfulfilled religious symphony which was to have been a 'Death-Dance of Principles'. The theme of *Die Jakobsleiter*, in Schoenberg's own words, is 'how the man of today, who has passed through materialism, socialism and anarchy, who was an atheist but has still preserved a remnant of ancient beliefs (in the form of superstition)—how this modern man struggles with God (see also "Jacob Wrestling" by Strindberg) and finally arrives at the point of finding God and becoming religious. How to learn to pray!'* Schoenberg had planned to complete

* *Arnold Schoenberg: Letters*, p. 35.

the cycle of birth, death and re-incarnation embodied in *Die Jakobsleiter* by setting the final chapter ('Journey to Heaven') of Balzac's *Seraphita*, a project also of Alban Berg's. In fact, as in fiction, though, the 'journey into hell' (which *Die Jakobsleiter* contains) could be superbly done, while the 'journey to heaven' remained an unrealizable dream.

It is quite probable that *Die Jakobsleiter* did furnish important ideas for the Mann-Leverkühn oratorio, for Schoenberg turned once more to work on *Die Jakobsleiter* in 1944 while Mann was engaged on *Faustus* and the two men were still friends. More conclusively, we have Schoenberg's word that he sent Mann a copy of *Die Jakobsleiter* (presumably only of the text), 'with a nice dedication'. When the post-publication controversy broke out, Schoenberg complained that Mann had described *Die Jakobsleiter*'s 'religious poetry' as 'not fully brewed'.* Since we know that Mann 'stole' Leverkühn's String Trio directly from one of Schoenberg's completed works, we may guess that he would have had few scruples about transplanting ingredients for the *Apocalypsis* from *Die Jakobsleiter*.

Although the *Apocalypsis* is an exploration of ultimate chaos, the work itself is most strictly constructed. In his 12-tone Method Leverkühn has discovered the law by which apparent disorder may be transformed into comprehensible, self-sufficient, artistic construction. Here Mann develops his theme of the artistic and political barbarity that is induced by the irrational adoption of a totalitarian principle, and of the once-and-for-all commitment to this principle which is taken as sufficient reason for the suspension of further moral (or aesthetic) scrutiny. The 'essential point', Mann said, was 'to make

* Article by Schoenberg in *Music Survey*, 1949, Vol. II, No. 2.

the opus open simultaneously to the criticism of bloody barbarism and to the criticism of bloodless intellectualism' (GN, 126). It was to be a two-fold attack, first on the 'worship of the unconscious, the glorification of its dynamic as the only life-promoting force, the systematic glorification of the primitive and irrational' (E3D, 416), and secondly, on the irresponsibilities, the not-wanting-to-know, of those German intellectuals and aesthetes who prepared the ground for the Third Reich.

In *Genesis* Mann describes how he approached Adorno for help with the long passages on the *Apocalypsis*, which he wanted to intertwine with a depiction by 'the good Serenus' of the whole unhealthy complex of anti-democratic post-war Germany, as represented by the 'arch-fascistic gatherings' of the Kridwiss circle—a Munich group of intellectuals who meet at the Schwabing house of Sixtus Kridwiss, a collector of east-Asiatic wood-carvings and an expert in the graphic arts.* Mann modulates smoothly from their table-talk—'a cold-blooded intellectual commentary upon a fervid experience of art and friendship' (571)—to a description of the composition of the *Apocalypsis*, which was written in

> a state of mind which, no longer interested in the psycho-
> logical, pressed for the objective, for a language that
> expressed the absolute, the binding and compulsory, and

* The members of the circle were modelled on real persons whom Mann had known in Munich either before, or shortly after the War. Sixtus Kridwiss is probably intended as a portrait of Emil Preetorius, remembered today for his Wagner stage designs, and then president of the Bavarian Academy of Fine Arts. The other putative 'originals' of the circle include Georg Habich, who was director of the Munich Numismatic Collection, Joseph Nadler, the literary historian and fervent nationalist, Stefan George's disciple Ludwig Derleth, the Jewish scholar Oskar Goldberg, and Edgar Dacqué, a professor of paleontology. Gunilla Bergsten documents the Kridwiss 'originals' in some detail, see GBF, 27–34.

in consequence by choice laid on itself the pious fetters of
pre-classically strict form.   (372)

'What I have vaguely in mind', Mann wrote to Adorno,
'is something satanically religious, diabolically pious,
seeming at one and the same time strictly bound by form
and criminally irresponsible, frequently a mockery of art
itself; and also something that goes back to primitive,
elementary levels of music . . .' (GN, 122). Shortly after,
in live discussion, Mann and Adorno agreed that the
work should include the whole 'apocalyptic culture'
whose writings, Zeitblom tells us, were so drawn on by
Leverkühn as to

> assemble them in one pregnant, portentous synthesis,
> and in relentless transmission hold up to humanity the
> mirror of the revelation, that it might see therein what
> is oncoming and near at hand.   (356)

These apocalyptic writings include the fourth-century
Greek *Vision of St. Paul*, early Christian and medieval
accounts of visions and speculations about the other
world, texts by the mystics Hildegarde of Bingen and
Mechtild of Magdeburg, the Venerable Bede's *Historia
ecclesiastica gentis anglorum*, Ezekiel, the Revelation of
St John the Divine, the Psalms, the Apocrypha, the
Lamentations of Jeremiah–and Dante. The reader is
given little more than this catalogue and there is no
description of how this vast material was edited into a
satisfactory whole.

The key figure in the *Apocalypsis* is the narrator, who
sets himself objectively and amorally outside his story.
He is a tenor 'of almost castrato-like high register, whose
chilly crow, objective, reporter-like, stands in terrifying
contrast to the content of his catastrophic announce-
ments' (377). The device of setting a cool narrator

between the audience and the story has an honourable pedigree—as witness such diverse examples as the part of the Evangelist in the Bach Passions, the narrator in Japanese *Bunraku* theatre, the Dostoevskian narrator who never quite seems to understand the drift of events, and the black-tied Speaker in Stravinsky's *Oedipus Rex*, to say nothing of Zeitblom's own role.

Parody and self-parody abound in the *Apocalypsis* where, we are told, Leverkühn's

> capacity for mocking imitation . . . became creative here in the parody of the different musical styles in which the insipid wantonness of hell indulges: French impressionism is burlesqued, along with bourgeois drawing-room music, Tchaikovsky, music-hall, the syncopations and rhythmic somersaults of jazz—like a tilting ring it goes round and round, gaily glittering, above the fundamental utterance of the main orchestra, which, grave, sombre, and complex, asserts with radical severity the intellectual level of the work as a whole. (375–6)

What are we to make of all this, and what is it intended to tell us about Leverkühn? We may perhaps begin by considering the passage from Jeremiah which Leverkühn sets to a 'harsh choral fugue':

> Wherefore doth a living man complain
> A man for the punishment of his sins?
> Let us search and try out ways,
> And turn again to the Lord . . .
>
> We have transgressed and have rebelled:
> Thou has not pardoned.
> Thou hast covered with anger
> And persecuted us:
> Thou hast slain, thou hast not pitied. . . . (359)

Crystallized here is a conflict central to the idea of the *Apocalypsis*. Leverkühn is now torn between working his purpose out to the bitter end in the belief that his sin is already beyond hope of expiation, and recanting, in the faith that it is *never* too late to 'turn again to the Lord'. The former alternative is complicated by his argument, in the dialogue with the devil, that 'the true theological way to salvation' lies in

> the *contritio* without hope, . . . the rocklike firm con-
> viction of the sinner that he has done too grossly for even
> the Everlasting Goodness to be able to forgive his sin.
> . . . (247)

Behind this also lingers the Nietzschean notion (as once expounded by Erich Heller) that having claimed his victim, the devil would envy the extremity of Lever-kühn's capacity for suffering and so kick him out—into heaven. In the dialogue at least it is the devil who wins, albeit on a somewhat obscure point, with his argument that 'the conscious speculation on the charm which great guilt exercises on Goodness makes the act of mercy to the uttermost unpossible to it' (247). We are therefore not surprised to find the second part of the *Apocalypsis* beginning with a children's chorus,—'inaccessibly un-earthly and alien beauty of sound, filling the heart with longing without hope . . . in its musical essence, for him who has ears to hear and eyes to see, the devil's laughter all over again'.* The finale, 'so far from being a roman-tic music of redemption, relentlessly confirms the theologically negative and pitiless character of the whole' (360).

*   *   *

---

* 'No people sing with such pure voices as those who live in deepest Hell; what we take for the song of angels is their song.' From an unpublished letter of Kafka's, quoted by Erich Heller in *The Disinherited Mind*, p. 202.

Mann reports in *Genesis* how struck he had been by the extent to which John of Patmos borrowed from other visionaries and ecstatics – and how in general the victim of hallucination traditionally drew upon fixed visions and experiences. 'I was struck, as the text [i.e., of *Faustus*] puts it, by the fact "that a raving man should rave in the same pattern as another who came before him; that one is ecstatic not independently, so to speak, but by rote" .'* This idea bears a marked affinity to the Nietzschean 'eternal recurrence'. Zeitblom refers to

> the track round the sphere . . . on which regress and progress, the old and the new, past and future, become one—
> I saw it all realized here, in a regression full of modern novelty, going back beyond Bach's and Handel's harmonic art to the remoter part of true polyphony. (372)

He remarks on the characteristic combination of the very new and the very old,

> but surely this is by no means an arbitrary combination; rather it lies in the nature of things: it rests, I might say, on the curvature of the world, which makes the last return unto the first. (376)

We may even perhaps see the *Apocalypsis* as a representation of a complete circuit of a cycle of eternal recurrence. There are choruses which begin as 'speaking' and

> by stages, by the way of the most extraordinary transitions, turn into the richest vocal music; then choruses which pass through all the stages from graded whisperings, antiphonal speech, and humming up to the most polyphonic song – accompanied by sounds which begin as

---

* Mann added that he recognized his own growing inclination 'to look upon all life as a cultural project taking the form of mythic cliches, and to prefer quotation to independent invention. *Faustus* shows many a trace of this leaning' (GN, 125).

mere noise, like tom-toms and thundering gongs, savage, fanatical, ritual, and end by arriving at the purest music. (373)

Here is a work to end works (a modern preoccupation from Scriabin right down to Jean Barraqué with his self-dedication to a 'terminal' composition based on Hermann Broch's *The Death of Virgil*), a desperate final circuit of the music cycle—the product, like virtually all such unlimited enterprises, of a panic-stricken narcissism. What is here imagined by Mann is a work whose language (and expressive range) runs the entire gamut from the simplest to the most complex statement imaginable. Further, the very birth from chaos of that language to its eventual running out are here charted.

The *Apocalypsis* may be seen not only as a complete circuit of a cycle of eternal recurrence, but also as showing a possible means of breaking that circuit, i.e., by accepting an altogether different set of values, in this case those which are the inverse of those formerly current. Now 'consonance and firm tonality are reserved for the world of hell' while 'dissonance stands for the expression of everything lofty, solemn, pious, everything of the spirit . . .' (375) .

'The reproach of barbarism', the knowledge of 'the theological almost exclusively as judgement and terror', the extolling of anarchy as order, the stressing of the close association of aestheticism and barbarism ('in the searing, susurrant tones of spheres and angels there is not one note which does not occur, with rigid correspondence, in the hellish laughter' (379)—what we have here is not so much the Nietzschean transvaluation of values, but rather an intermediate, transitional stage of the inversion of previously accepted values, a stage recognized by Nietzsche himself: 'I have the gift of *reversing perspectives*: the first reason why it is perhaps for me alone that a "revaluation of values" is at all possible today' (NK, 659). His reversed perspectives included the inversion of accepted causalities, the devaluation of the primacy of faith, throwing emphasis on instinct rather than reason, on the subjective rather than the objective, and a claim 'to see *healthier* concepts and values in the perspective of the sick' (NK, 658).

And thus with Leverkühn. 'In whom will you recognize theological existence if not in me?' asks the devil (243).* Where order had once reigned, there one would extol chaos, where reason, unreason, where discipline, anarchy, where sanity, madness, where truth, untruth: 'an untruth of a kind that enhances power holds its own against any ineffectively virtuous truth'. Where warmth and love, coldness; it was a 'flight from the cold of a loveless life into the fires of creation'. Where humanity, inhumanity; ' "Has your music been inhuman up to now?" ', asks the violinist Rudi Schwerdtfeger, ' "then it owes its greatness to its inhumanity" ' (456). So, symbolically, consonance and tonality come to be reserved for the demonic, dissonance and atonality for the alarming glimpses of light which break through from time to time.

'Going to school to the devil' means not only embracing every kind of principle contrary to whatever was previously accepted, but erecting disorder as the new principle of order. And the devil's lesson is, 'There is no order save

---

* cf. an idea of Ivan Karamazov: 'for every individual . . . who does not believe in God or immortality, the moral law of nature must immediately be changed into the exact contrary of the former religious law, and . . . egoism, even to crime, must become not only lawful but even recognized as the inevitable, the most rational, even honourable outcome of the position'. *The Brothers Karamazov*, op. cit., Vol. 1, p. 66.

disorder; this is our experience and so be it', the ultimate perversion being the invocation of a law to generate, to approve disorder as such. A categorical statement of 'thus it is' offers itself as a principle by which chaos may disport itself to the greatest effect.

*　　　*　　　*

It is worth recalling here an earlier episode in Leverkühn's life where Mann had taken the opportunity to air various fears about the dehumanization and abstraction of art. Leverkühn tells of his adventures with 'an American scholar named Akercocke,* in company with whom he was supposed to have set up a new deep-sea record' (267). Together, Leverkühn would have Zeitblom believe, they descended into the depths of the ocean and from the diving-bell marvelled at the uncanny creatures to be found there. Leverkühn had spoken of his itch

> to expose the unexposed, to look at the unlooked-at, the not-to-be and not-expecting-to-be looked-at. There was a feeling of indiscretion, even of guilt, bound up with it, not quite allayed by the feeling that science must be allowed to press just as far forwards as it is given the intelligence of scientists to go. (268)

Zeitblom's account conveys a feeling of trespass, of disobedience, of improper studies. Leverkühn had enjoyed glimpses into a world whose soundless, frantic foreignness was, he said, 'explained and even justified by its utter lack of contact with our own' (267). He was no less forward in astro-physical science. Indeed it appeared to Zeitblom that Professor Akercocke had not only been down in the darkness of the ocean deeps with him, but also up among the stars . . . Thus Leverkühn arrived at

---

* 'Capercailzie' in the original German. There is no apparent reason why the translator, H. T. Lowe-Porter, chose to change the name.

'measures, figures, orders of greatness with which the human spirit has no longer any relation, and which lose themselves in the theoretic and abstract, in the entirely non-sensory, not to say non-sensical' (266).

These journeyings in search of knowledge and the fantastic are Faust's traditional excursions with Mephisto, and they echo the attitude of the sixteenth-century Faust chapbook toward forbidden knowledge, an attitude which Mann, with his conservative attitude to art and its proper concerns, partly shared. Mann felt that the post-Renaissance humanist culture was running down, the process being accelerated not least by those very scientific, coolly objective modes of thought which Leverkühn preferred to those of a warmer, more immediate humanity. Where then could one go from here? How far was the 'air from other planets' * which Schoenberg and Stefan George had found so exhilarating, generally available? For Mann this sort of exploration incurred a sense of violation and guilt. Of Leverkühn's trip to the deeps, Zeitblom writes:

> The incredible eccentricities, some grisly, some comic, which nature here achieved, forms and features which seemed to have scarcely any connection with the upper world but rather belong to another planet: these were the product of seclusion, sequestration, of reliance on being wrapped in eternal darkness.   (268)

Not for Zeitblom Jean Cocteau's view that 'the poet, whose range is unlimited, sometimes brings back a pearl from depths into which the man of science *proves* it is impossible to descend'.†

* Words from the first line of George's poem 'Entrückung' ('Rapture') set by Schoenberg in the exploratory atonal fourth movement of his Second String Quartet (1908).

† *A Call to Order*, translated by R. H. Myers, Faber and Gwyer, London, 1926, p. 168.

To behold the wonders of the deeps one had to descend in a strong diving-bell, painfully aware of the precariousness of the venture—some hundreds of thousands of tons of water-pressure bearing upon the vessel. (To breathe the new air one would presumably need the stratospheric balloon to which Professor Akercocke/Capercailzie's diving-bell is compared.) The bell enabled one to observe but also to remain aloof from the strange sights of the world outside, which remained impenetrably alien because of the physical limitations of our humanity. New worlds of feeling (and art) might indeed exist, but how far were they available? Could they really be integrated into our experience or must they remain as incredible curiosities? Mann's view here seems to be that they must, for to bring the creatures of the deeps back alive to sea-level 'one would have to preserve for them while ascending the same tremendous atmospheric pressure they were used to and adapted to in their environment'. The essence of the metaphor is Mann's familiar theme that certain areas of experience are only accessible to art through the loss of humanity. His construction of the real historical situation was that the journeys to the deeps, the flights to the stars, were but demonic perversions, cultivations of the outlandish for its own sensational sake, futile explorations of territory that could never yield proper substance for art.

But an important part of Mann's concern here was that the direct world of human experience and feeling was being too easily dismissed. It seemed to him that overreaching into the disorders of extra-human experiences was being preferred to attempts at a deeper understanding of the human condition. We are intended to take note of the possible dehumanization of art, of its concerning itself with regions so obscure and inaccessible as to be denied to all but those with private diving-bells or stratospheric balloons.

*   *   *

These images of height and depth convey a reaching out to the furthest limits and beyond. They are closely associated and mirror each other. The 'altus' leitmotif, extensively developed in this episode, makes frequent appearance in *Faustus* and is particularly effective in the description of the *Apocalypsis*. It appears there as the note for note correspondence between the music of the angelic chorus and that of the laughter of hell. Leverkühn characteristically chooses the highest and the lowest but never the space between with its definitive mediocrity and humanity. Yet in psychological perspective this is a condition which has already turned the corner back towards health. This is particularly significant in so far as Leverkühn is representative of 'the German Problem'. 'With my patients', wrote Jung,

> the *katabasis* [psychic collapse] and *katalysis* [dissolution] are followed by a recognition of the bipolarity of human nature and the necessity of conflicting pairs of opposites. After the symbols of madness experienced during the period of disintegration there follow images which represent the coming together of opposites; light/dark, above/below, white/black, male/female, etc. (JSM, 140)

Mann himself was more familiar with Freud and, as we saw in the previous chapter, in his essay on the psychologist he quotes Freud's view of how contradictory stimuli co-existing in the id can unite in compromise forms which ensure a high efficiency of energy release. Mann then adds his own interpretation of how 'in the historical experience of our own day' this phenomenon

I

can take the upper hand with ego, with a whole mass-ego, thanks to a moral devastation which is produced by worship of the unconscious, the glorification of its dynamic as the only life-promoting force, the systematic glorification of the primitive and irrational.   (E3D, 416)

The way forward from here, he said, drawing on Freud again, was through analysis: to rob certain archetypal wish stimuli buried in the id of their charge of energy by bringing them to consciousness. The path to a healthier future is defined. It would lead to new 'psychological man' who would have passed comfortably and understandingly through the Pandora's box stage of the id, and to whom a new humanity and a new art would be born. Mann foresees

> a humanism of the future, which we dimly divine and which will have experienced much that the earlier humanism knew not of. It will be a humanism standing in a different relation to the powers of the lower world, the unconscious, the id: a relation, bolder, freer, blither, productive of a riper art than any possible in our neurotic fear-ridden, hate-ridden world.   (E3D, 427)

The conversion of our great fear and our great hate into a different relation to the unconscious would, Mann hoped, one day be due to the healing effect of Freud's discoveries, and the new relation would be 'more the artist's, more ironic and yet not necessarily irreverent . . .'. One only wishes Mann had defined this relation and his concept of psychological man rather more exactly. It is hard to resist the comment that Mann's analytical and retrospective insights were of a far higher order than his long range forecasts. His penchant for ironic evaluation proved stronger than his wholly sincere efforts to think constructively about the future, to anticipate its difficulties and attempt to meet them. This is an enigma to which we shall return in our final chapter.

*   *   *

Prior to writing the *Apocalypsis*, Leverkühn's health had taken an unusually severe turn for the worse: 'It was as though he were pinched and plagued with hot pincers . . .' (341). These pains are of course syphilitic in origin, as Mann's clinically exact description makes plain, and they represent those of the creator's necessary wound. They are the artist's sacrifice, part and parcel of the renunciation of a 'normal' human life. In Leverkühn's case Mann deliberately leaves one in doubt whether they are birth pangs of the New, or merely punishment for improper studies. Leverkühn himself is well aware of the significance of his sufferings, and he draws Zeitblom's attention (just as the devil had previously drawn his) to Hans Andersen's fairy story about the little mermaid, who, 'perhaps to win, like human beings, an immortal soul' (343), willingly endured the cruel pains of exchanging her fish's tail for human legs. Leverkühn 'uncommonly loved and admired' the mermaid, calling her 'his sister in affliction' (344). In the same spirit that she was ready to bear the knife-sharp pains that accompanied every step with her new white legs, so Leverkühn accepts the burden of pain associated with the unnatural infection he has embraced for the sake of his art. In the same way that she gambles her natural being on a generally unobtainable prize, so Leverkühn signs away his own body and mind. And the outcome of his enterprise is at this stage no less certain than hers.

A doctor called in not by him but by Frau Schweigestill prescribes a ludicrously impertinent series of remedies, all

of them useless, whereon Leverkühn reaffirms his con-
viction 'that he, more or less alone, out of his own
nature and powers, would have to get rid of the evil'
(345).

But before he is able to attempt to do so by projecting
it into the *Apocalypsis*, an action which miraculously lifts
the illness from him, the young and famous concert
violinist Rudi Schwerdtfeger puts in an unwelcome
appearance and encouraged by the darkness and inhumanity of Leverkühn's room tempts him, for the
present unsuccessfully, to waver from his purpose.

Schwerdtfeger, who is not a whit put out by Leverkühn's coolness toward him, and zealously concerns
himself with Leverkühn's condition, represents all-too-
human humanity—he is the personification of Leverkühn's suppressed humanity. As Zeitblom has it, 'He
[Schwerdtfeger] gave himself credit for an initiative that
belonged entirely to the other party . . .' (416). He is the
Aaron whose eloquence is but a reproach to the idea of
Moses which it strives to convey. His specifications to
Leverkühn for the violin concerto which he wants to
commission show that he knows precisely what will work
in terms of accepted values. As communicator, as com-
promiser, he is a serious threat to Leverkühn's purpose,
but although he gains a little ground, he pays dearly for it
and cannot deflect Leverkühn from his chosen course. He
wins both the Violin Concerto (1924, and first performed
in Vienna in that year) and the longed for *per Du* with
Leverkühn; but to do so he has come too close and is
punished for it. Even his tactics are imperfectly conceived; '. . . he was illogical enough to use his native gift
of coquetry—and then to feel put off when the melancholy preference he aroused did not lack the signs of
ironic eroticism' (415). Nevertheless it was clear to Zeit-

blom that 'the victim [Leverkühn] did not see that he
had been bewitched' (416).

The further Leverkühn plunges into inhuman enterprise, the greater the temptations of straightforward
humanity, with consequent intensification of his pains as
he yields to those temptations. For every flicker of
warmth, every glimmer of redemption, he pays dearly.

After completion of the *Apocalypsis*, he writes
Schwerdtfeger the promised Concerto, only to have the
violinist betray him when sent as his Rosenkavalier to
the black-eyed Marie Godeau (probably modelled on the
dark lady of the Sonnets), whom he had hoped to win for
himself. A double betrayal this, for he who had plighted
himself to a loveless life that the creative fires might burn
the fiercer, would here have taken a wife, no matter how
unlikely the match. It is a story unmistakably reminiscent
of Nietzsche's unsuccessful suit to Lou Salomé *via*
Paul Rée.

Kindled more than a little by his work on the Violin
Concerto, Leverkühn contemplates marrying the stage
designer Marie Godeau in whom he recognizes (as he has
failed to do so in Schwerdtfeger) a possible humanizing
complement to his world of 'musical theology, oratorio, mathematical number-magic' (423). Dreading the
declaration of his feelings, he confides in the violinist his
desire for 'a warmer and more human atmosphere
around him . . . most of all because he hopes to get from
it good and fine things for his working energy and
enthusiasm, for the human content of his future work'
(436), and so asks that he should bear his proposal to
Marie.

But Schwerdtfeger (here, a true disciple of Genet's
dictum, 'only incomplete actions are vile') turns on him:
'Has your music been inhuman up till now? Then it owes

its greatness to its inhumanity. Forgive the simplicity of the remark, but I would not want to hear any humanly inspired work from you' (436). Truly, one might think, this is but Leverkühn conversing with himself—arguing that Olympian, supra-human achievement is only possible through being bold enough to be inhuman—but so intent is Leverkühn on the matter in hand that he dismisses the objection as impertinent, coming as it does from 'the very person who had the amazing patience to win me over for the human and persuaded me to say *Du*; the person in whom for the first time in my life I found human warmth'. As so often happens, that which would tempt us from our purposes has the keenest appreciation of their value.

Even when Schwerdtfeger confesses (hardly surprisingly) that he too is interested in Marie, Leverkühn persists in sending him—and the inevitable happens. In taking up with Marie, however, Schwerdtfeger betrays not only Leverkühn but also his (Schwerdtfeger's) mistress Inez Rodde, daughter of the senator's widow with whom Leverkühn had lodged in Munich between 1910 and 1912.* Inez's husband, Helmut Institoris, is described as 'that rather limited teacher of aesthetics, wrapped in his dreams of beauty and brutality' (327). Inez herself, refined and pensive, a seeker out of bourgeois security and values, has one important thing in common with Leverkühn in that through her affair with Schwerdtfeger she shows herself prepared to sacrifice herself for 'one sweet, indispensable triumph'. Thus her betrayal parallels and reinforces Leverkühn's. But it is left to Inez to avenge the betrayer. Riding home in the

---

* Inez was modelled on Mann's sister Julia who, although she too committed suicide, did so out of *ennui* rather than as a consequence of a *crime passionel*: see GBF, 21.

tram from Schwerdtfeger's farewell concert in Munich, Inez empties a revolver into her faithless lover.

Worse still is to come, for the love with which Leverkühn responds to his little nephew Nepomuk—an unexpected final ray of light before the darkness closes in—is rewarded by the boy's death. It is a death so cruel that Leverkühn curses his devil and resolves that the time for *his* betrayal is now at hand.

CHAPTER EIGHT

The Lamentation of Doctor Faustus

Leverkühn's last work, *Dr. Fausti Weheklag*, the *Lamentation of Dr. Faustus*, is already taking shape in his mind, when, in a brief and tragic episode, he feels once more, and now more intensely than ever before, the warmth of the forbidden human love. Zeitblom notices that he had written on one of his papers: 'This sadnesse moved Dr. Faustum that he made note of his lament-acyon'. This 'sadnesse' is Leverkühn's response to the death of his five-year-old nephew, the angelic Nepomuk Scheidewein, his companion for a mere month or two in the summer of 1928 when 'Echo', as he was known, had come to convalesce at Pfeiffering after a severe attack of measles.* Was it because he, the man to whom love was denied, had again dared to love, that his punishment must be shared by the object of his love? Incensed at this further betrayal, the devil determines that the child shall die. Never before is Leverkühn so moved as by the child's horribly painful illness (cerebro-spinal meningitis – and one notices the similarity to the infection which all this time has been merely skirmishing as yet in the composer's brain), and he curses his devil:

'I thought he would concede this much, after all, maybe just this; but no, where should he learn mercy, who is

* Echo's appearance and personality (though not his untimely end!) were modelled on Mann's grandson Fridolin (b. 1940), son of Gret (Moser) and Michael Mann (b. 1919).

without any bowels of compassion? Probably it was just
exactly this he had to crush in his beastly fury. Take him,
scum, filth, excrement!' he shrieked. . . . 'What a sin,
what a crime . . . that we let him come, that I let him
be near me, that I feasted my eyes on him! You must
know that children are tender stuff, they are receptive
for poisonous influences.' (477–8)

To which Zeitblom replies: 'It may rend our hearts but
must not rob us of our reason. You have done nothing
but loving-kindness to him . . .' Leverkühn turns on the
complacent comfortable-mindedness, that hiding from
the real nature of things which it has been the chosen
task of our modern age to expose. Shocked and moved
more than he could have imagined possible, stung out of
the small corner of humanity he had always left for
himself, he finds the few sharp words he needs:

> 'I find,' he said, 'that it is not to be.'
> 'What, Adrian, is not to be?'
> 'The good and noble,' he answered me; 'what we call
> the human, although it is good, and noble. What human
> beings have fought for and stormed citadels, what the
> ecstatics exultantly announced—that is not to be. It will
> be taken back. I will take it back.'
> 'I don't quite understand, dear man. What will you
> take back?'
> 'The Ninth Symphony,' he replied. And then no more
> came, though I waited for it.   (478)

How aptly Mann chooses late Beethoven to set against
late Leverkühn! Beethoven, frustrated in his everyday
need for human warmth and friendship, yet sustained by
his vision of all men as brothers, turned to Schiller's
'Ode to Joy' for the Ninth Symphony.

At the time of writing, Mann was reading *The Tempest*, that haven reached by Shakespeare where, after due
trial and torment, all can be forgiven, all will at last be

well. Thus we are not surprised to find Leverkühn, immediately prior to his *Lamentation*, setting Ariel's songs. Doubtless *The Tempest* was especially attractive to Mann because of his life-long doubts about art and the artist; for Prospero drowns his book, buries his staff certain fathoms in the earth and abjures 'this rough magic' for his own 'faint' but natural strength and a retirement 'where every third thought shall be my grave'. But for Leverkühn it is not to be. Now, with Ivan Karamazov and those in Camus's *La Peste* watching the death of another child, he is sure that there is no God. There is nothing further to deter him from fulfilment of his pact because, with Faust, the hero of his *Lamentation*, 'he despises the positivism of the world for which one would save him, the lie of its godliness'. He must and will be true to his experience, and that experience dictates that all he has left to utter is lament. Enough of the evasions offered by parody and irony, of ambiguity, of the insistence that the scale of values does not suffer if stood on its head (as in the *Apocalypsis*). Leverkühn can no longer refuse to choose. And he chooses darkness now not for its own sake but because he believes either that there is no light, or that it is withheld.

The resolution of choice and the discovery of a language to express what he has chosen are convergent. In recognizing what he had in fact chosen some twenty-four years before, that *then* he had chosen the dark path, he finds the language to express what he felt before he made his pact with the devil. What he had felt then he had not dared acknowledge, so that his career as an artist had been nothing more than an evasion, the bargain being that if he kept faith the evasion would be complete. Yet in the *Lamentation* he breaks the pact, for here he summons every technical resource at his command not to overrule but to serve an eruption of human feeling which he no longer has the power to deny. By the expression of his lament that the good is not to be, and by his exposure of the lie of the world's godliness, he revokes not only the idea of transcendent reality, but also, unwittingly, his pact with the devil. For, albeit subject to the strictest law, he here pours out his feelings, whereas before they had been suppressed; personal emotion had been frozen so that forbidden stimulants and technique alone might generate the appearance of feeling as, for instance, in the Violin Concerto. And so too with Mann himself, who in *Doctor Faustus* had not been content merely to play with his material but had himself entered into it more closely than he had ever done before.

The subject matter of the *Lamentation* is the Faust legend itself, and specifically the version of the first chapbook, the *Urfaustbuch*. This is often drawn on word for word in the description of Leverkühn's composition. The Faust of Leverkühn's oratorio follows Urfaust; in both versions, the last request Faust makes to his friends is that they do not watch with him but rather get themselves quietly to their beds to sleep. In both versions, too, Faust dies 'as a bad and as a good Christian' hoping that the sufferings of the body at the hands of the devil may be so terrible as to win ultimate redemption for the soul. Just as the process of creation is always, in some shape or form, reflected in the finished work of art, so we find the Faust in Mann seeking the Faust in Leverkühn who, in his supreme composition, seeks out the archetype, the Urfaust whose story is his story. Mann's debt to the Faust myth and the significance of his recasting of it have already been touched on and I shall return to this again in the next chapter.

Leverkühn's music, we are told, lasts an hour and a quarter (the approximate duration of the Ninth Symphony). It is entirely in variation form permeated by a 12-note kernel, 'out of which everything develops'. The kernel appears in its basic form at the words ' "For I die as a bad and as a good Christian" '–this being a direct quotation from the *Urfaustbuch*. But even more fundamental, we are told, is the 5-note motif, B, E, A, E, E-Flat, whose significance will by now be familiar. This motif governs both melody and harmony 'everywhere where there is reference to the bond and the vow, the promise and the blood pact'. Leverkühn dies 'good' in that he has been true to his experience, which for him (the idea of a second Fall, denial of love, etc.) had to be 'bad'. Despising the lie of the world's godliness, he had carried through his belief that 'an untruth of a kind which enhances power holds its own against any ineffectively virtuous truth'. The idea that 'out of the sheerly irremediable, hope might germinate' is not Leverkühn's, who believes that he has gambled and lost. The attempt to challenge God, to outrage him into putting in an appearance, has failed. There is no God. He is dead. Leverkühn is not at all indifferent to this; it is because it matters so profoundly to him that he undertakes his journey into the interior in the first place. Nietzsche argued his death of God on the ground not so much that he actually knew him to be dead but rather that he believed that before we deserve a God we must have shown we can do without him.

The important 'altus' idea from the *Apocalypsis* of the congruence of the musics of heaven and hell reappears in the *Lamentation*. The perfect thematic unity of the whole ensures that even the most diverse elements are always related. There is no longer 'any free note'.

Totalitarian authority has always been able to make out a plausible case for black being white and white black. As the *Lamentation* is dedicated to the revocation, the un-writing of Beethoven's Ninth Symphony, it is negatively related to it in that the choral writing gives way before a purely orchestral adagio; we know that Mann himself was not fond of the choral finale of the Ninth (see GN, 178). The adagio begins after Faust has summoned his friends, warned them that his end is at hand and bidden them sleep in peace, for his sorrow lies beyond words and past all consolation. This is intended not only to echo the *Urfaustbuch*, but also to be 'the conscious and deliberate reversal of the "Watch with me" of Geth-semane'. For the concluding 'Ode to Sorrow', for the extreme lament, nothing will serve but 'the speaking unspokenness given to music alone'; here, 'the final despair achieves a voice'.

The descent into hell is portrayed in 'an orgy of in-fernal jollity', reminiscent of the parodistic fifth move-ment of Berlioz's *Symphonie Fantastique* and of the mood of the *Apocalypsis*. As another contrast to the static and mournful nature of the whole, there is a choral scherzo where 'the evil spirit sets to at the gloomy Faustus with strange mocking jests and sayings'. Orchestral interludes, which are sometimes reflections of the general theme and are sometimes dramatic (standing for parts of the plot) separate the choral passages. It is possible to read the description of the *Lamentation* as a description of *Faustus* itself* and it may be that the 'orchestral interludes' are intended to refer back, corresponding to the part played in the structure of the novel by the descriptions of Leverkühn's musical compositions, while the 'choral passages' correspond to the rest of the text. A feature of

* For a thoroughgoing demonstration of this, see GBF, 179–200.

the *Lamentation* is the punning inclusion (which works more tellingly in German than in English) of its first cause, the death of the little boy:

> The echo, the giving back of the human voice as nature-sound, and the revelation of it *as* nature-sound, is essentially a lament: Nature's melancholy 'Alas!' in view of man, her effort to utter his solitary state. . . . In Leverkühn's last and loftiest creation, echo, favourite device of the baroque, is employed with unspeakably mournful effect. (486)

But the most important idea behind the *Lamentation* is that 'just by virtue of the absoluteness of the form the music is, as language, freed' (488). Extreme calculation liberates the purely expressive, here, 'in its first and original manifestation, expressiveness as lament'. Going further, Zeitblom suggests that 'all expressiveness is really lament', and he appeals for evidence to Monteverdi.* Feeling is thereby restored to music, Zeitblom speculates, and although unsuspected by the composer himself, the longed for breakthrough is achieved.

Many of Leverkühn's earlier compositions are also strictly composed, but we are given to understand that the *Lamentation* is the most rigorous of all and that it is precisely because this rigour is *absolute* that the language is 'freed' and once more at the service of natural expression. This is not at all an easy idea to construe, for

---

* As Monteverdi strove deliberately for an 'expressive' style, he is not a very apt example. Expressiveness does indeed appear at its finest as 'lament' in his work, but it is a misrepresentation to suggest that this expressiveness was liberated by extreme calculation. 'The long-standing hold of this "impersonal" theory about the sixteenth century', writes Wilfrid Mellers, 'is certainly curious when one remembers the avowedly expressive intentions of many of the composers . . . chromaticisms represent love, death and pain, melismatic passages flower out of reference to physical movement.' (*Music and Society*, Dennis Dobson, London, 1946, p. 54.)

until now the dominant idea has been the culpability of adopting a totally strict, generative, order and then exercising no further control over the content, which, it was implied, is the product of the untamed stimuli of the id. But, as we have seen, this time there is conscious deliberation behind the content—the expression of Leverkühn's lament for the child—and thus at last the rigour of system becomes a means not of generating the appearance of feeling, but of ordering feeling into art, the extremity of feeling demanding an equally extreme control if the subjective is to translate itself into the objective and universal. Leverkühn's position, as will soon be evident, is here close to that of Schoenberg.

Zeitblom's wild assertion that all expression (presumably he means 'in art') is really lament is scarcely proven, but it acquires specific meaning if we ask Nietzsche's question: 'is it the *hatred* against life or the *excess* of life which has here become creative? In Goethe, for example, the excess became creative; in Flaubert, hatred . .' (NK, 671)—for there can be no doubt in which spirit Leverkühn's composition is conceived. The generality of Zeitblom's assertion was surely set down by Mann with Schopenhauer in mind. Schopenhauer praised tragedy as the truest dramatic art; for him it was the truest statement of 'how things are'—'the terrible side of life . . . the unspeakable pain, the ills of humanity, the triumph of evil, the scornful domination of chance, and the irretrievable fall of the just and innocent'.* The core of Mann's thought here is that in Leverkühn's fallen state, the only proper and sincere expression for him is lament: the composer has divined the truth of the devil's original contention that 'Only the non-fictional is still

---

* *The World as Will and Idea*, translated by R. B. Haldane and J. Kemp, London, 1888, Vol. 1, p. 326.

permissible, the unplayed, the undisguised and untrans-
figured expression of suffering in its actual moment'
(240).

*   *   *

In the many passages where the possibility of a breakthrough is discussed, Mann looks forward to a day when
the direct expression of feeling would once more be
possible. The language would have been revitalized, not
through the discovery of some unexpected new vocabulary, but through technical and moral mastery. One
might compare what Mann calls 'a stage of intellectuality
and formal strictness' (485) to the filter put up by linguistic philosophers to sort out honest from dishonest
usage of language. To reinvoke the Schoenbergian model,
Erich Heller has pointed out that

> There even is a family resemblance between the logical
> structures, motives and intentions of Wittgenstein's
> *Tractatus* and those of Schoenberg's musical theory; for
> Schoenberg too is guided by the conviction that the
> 'language' of his medium, music, has to be raised to that
> level of logical necessity which would eliminate all
> subjective accidents.   (HAJ, 209)

And so we are to imagine the language cleansed; for
the *Lamentation* ends with all the instruments retiring
one by one until finally we are left with a single note, that
high G on the cello, a sound more eloquent than any of
the foregoing orgy of diverse complexity. It is instructive
to compare this sense of an ending, of a fiction properly
complete, with the triumph of Schoenberg's expressionist
search when, at the end of his opera *Moses und Aron*, he
paradoxically finds his credo even as Moses thinks he has
lost his: 'O Wort, du Wort, das mir fehlt' ('O Word,
Word that I lack'). But there it is in the music—the high
sustained single note on the violins—'one is left with a

mere intimation of the kind of speech that may be possible there, where silence reigns' (Rilke).*

It is worth noticing that the possibility of break-through, if discussed with some measure of optimism, is realized as no more than a glimmer in Leverkühn's work, and then only in this final composition. Mann reports that he was at great pains to ensure that the 'ray of hope, the possibility of grace', was no more than that. His first attempt at the description of the ending of the *Lamentation* had, he acknowledged, 'kindled too much light, had been too lavish with the consolation' (GN, 176).

In the finished version there is offered no consolation other than the final despair achieving a voice. Any hope would be 'but a hope beyond hopelessness, the tran-scendence of despair–not betrayal to her, but the miracle that passes belief'. We are left with 'the high G of a cello,

---

* Quoted by J. B. Leishman in his introduction (p. 21) to Rainer Maria Rilke, *Duino Elegies*, translated by Leishman and Stephen Spender, The Hogarth Press, 1963. It is sometimes suggested, for instance by Robert Donington in his Jungian analysis of *Wagner's 'Ring' and its Symbols* (Faber, London, 1963) and by Wilfrid Mellers in his study of renewal in twentieth-century music (*Caliban Reborn*, Gollancz, London, 1960), that the dissolution of the musical texture at the end of such works as *The Ring*, Delius's *A Village Romeo and Juliet* and Schoenberg's *Erwartung*, symbolizes the potential of a new birth. Bearing in mind the novel's debts to Schoenberg, it is particularly interesting that Mellers (discussing *Erwartung*) speculates that 'Schoenberg's music has demonstrated how the glimmer of faith is to be attained only by the relinquishment of consciousness, of corporal rhythm, of thematic definition and of harmonic volition'. He goes on to point out that 'This mystical interpretation of the release from consciousness acquires explicit form at the end of *Die Jakobsleiter*, the gigantic oratorio that was to be the consumation of Schoenberg's "free" phase, though it remained (significantly) unfinished. The ladder of the title is the link between dying mortality and some kind of reincarnation, and the final pages of the score describe a woman on her deathbed who, having ex-perienced the transition from life to death, floats upward, disem-bodied.' (*Caliban Reborn*, pp. 44–5.)

K

the last word, the last fainting sound, slowly dying in a pianissimo-fermata. Then nothing more: silence and night. But that tone which vibrates in the silence, which is no longer there, to which only the spirit hearkens, and which was the voice of mourning, is so no more. It changes its meaning; it abides as a light in the night' (491). Is this not Nietzsche's story of the man who sets out into the night, but the lamp he carries is on his back and lights the path he has had to make only for those coming after?

Leverkühn summons his friends to hear his confession. Deserting his familiar personality, he takes on that known only to himself and merely hinted at only in that note which had caught Zeitblom's eye. The company are embarrassed and frightened by this unmasking of an unsuspected inner demonism, perhaps even recognizing at some level of consciousness that they too had allowed themselves to become its agents. One by one they depart, until finally the composer is left alone but for the faithful Zeitblom, Schildknapp and four close women acquaintances. He makes his way to the piano as if to play through the *Lamentation*, whose score has stood open upon the rack throughout his address.

> We saw tears run down his cheeks and fall on the keyboard, wetting it, as he attacked the keys in a strongly dissonant chord. At the same time he opened his mouth as though to sing, but only a wail which will ring for ever in my ears broke from his lips. He spread out his arms, bending over the instrument and seeming about to embrace it,* when suddenly, as though smitten by a blow, he fell sideways from his seat and to the floor.   (503)

* Mann clearly intends the reader to recall the onset of Nietzsche's madness (1889), which was signalled by his collapse while embracing the neck of a horse which he had seen being flogged by a coachman. Further, the last phase of Leverkühn's life, like that of the philosopher (who died on August 25th, 1900), is a ten-year spell of insanity.

The year is 1930, the composer's time is up and the devil has duly exacted his toll: henceforth Leverkühn's existence is that of a vegetable. The paralytic stroke at the piano plunges him into twelve-hours unconsciousness, after which Schildknapp and Zeitblom take him to Munich, to a private clinic for nervous diseases. There his illness is diagnosed as a disease of the brain which must be left to run its course. After three months his mother returns with him to his first home. 'Once soaring in a giddy arc above an astonished world', the bold, defiant spirit now creeps broken 'back to his mother's arms. . . . She takes him back, the "poor, dear child," to her bosom, thinking nothing else than that he would have done better never to have gone away' (506). He dies in August 1940 while the holocaust which was played out in his own life envelops Germany itself.

*   *   *

The ending of Leverkühn's final composition would seem to be for Mann, if not for Leverkühn, an act of faith, a statement of marginal artistic and political optimism. But what are the political implications, and how valid is the musical metaphor for the political reality?

We have seen how Mann continually exhorted Germany to recognize the folly of her enthusiasm for the Reich. Reluctantly he came to accept that if this recognition were not forthcoming and Germany could not of her own volition exorcize the evil, then for her own good it would have to be exorcized for her by military defeat, and by the humiliation of that defeat. These ideas are expressed over and over again in Mann's wartime broadcasts to Germany and in Zeitblom's personal lamentations in *Doctor Faustus*. Yet we must remember that

Mann did not begin work on the chapters describing the *Apocalyptic Oratorio* until the new year of 1946 (GN, 124), work on the chapter describing the *Lamentation* being virtually complete by new year's day 1947 (GN, 178). Zeitblom's time of beginning on the *Lamentation* chapter is given as April 25th, 1945, by which time, as he says himself, the war was in its final stages and Germany's total defeat was inevitable. His description of these final stages, with which he begins the chapter, expresses both horror and self-identifying shame at the atrocities and inhumanities wrought in the name of the Reich:

> Is the sense of guilt quite morbid which makes one ask oneself the question how Germany, whatever her future manifestations, can ever presume to open her mouth in human affairs? . . . German human beings, tens of thousands, hundreds of thousands it is, who have perpetrated what humanity shudders at; and all that is German now stands forth as an abomination and a warning. How will it be to belong to a land whose history witnesses this hideous default; a land self-maddened, psychologically burnt-out, which quite understandably despairs of governing itself and thinks it for the best that it becomes a colony of foreign powers . . .   (481–2)

He goes on to ask, as Mann often did, whether Hitler's Reich was not 'in word and deed, anything but the distorted, vulgarized, besmirched symbol of a state of mind, a notion of world affairs which we must recognize as genuine and characteristic?' The defeated people now stand 'wild-eyed in face of the void' just because 'they have failed, failed horribly in their last and uttermost attempt to find the political form suited to their particular needs' (482).

It would be unlikely therefore if Leverkühn's *Lamen-*

tation were to have anything significant to say about the accomplished fact of Germany's defeat. If the *Apocalyptic Oratorio* was a paradigm of Germany, of German greatness, inwardness and musicality, and of the forces that would be unleashed should the 'genuine and characteristic' demonic impulse in her soul be insufficiently contained by artistic enterprise, and so escape into political form, what was there left to do in the *Lamentation* but for Zeitblom to suggest '(though only in the lowest whisper) that, out of the sheerly irremediable, hope might germinate?' (491). Mann's idea would seem to be that just as Leverkühn triumphs over his devil through cursing him and, in giving tongue to his own lament for his life and works, becomes for the first time capable of subjective feeling–in short, a person–so only the acknowledgment and free confession by the Germans of their crimes would open the way to a better future. No military defeat could achieve what was really required; only confession and penitence could exorcize the strain of evil.

We must, however, be sensible of the limits of the metaphor whereby the predicament of a modern artist is intended to stand for Germany's political difficulties and the psychology of the German people. Although this metaphor is certainly valid for the pathology of the German psyche, it is of strictly limited validity where the possibility of an artistic breakthrough appears. It was clear to Mann, writing shortly after the end of the war, that Germany had been so thoroughly destroyed that a new start of some kind was inevitable. The defeat of Nazi Germany had made it possible for a ray of hope to appear–no more, because of the fear that the exorcism of the evil might not have been complete. Yet the metaphor may be pressed no further because the ray of hope for art appears through Leverkühn's successful attempt to find the form, the extreme form he needed, while the equivalent political form had served only to liberate and encourage the grossly inhuman. It had proved catastrophic for Germany's political needs which, Mann considered, could be met only by a democracy freely chosen by a people come at last to political maturity. Leverkühn's deliberate self-infection, for example, is undertaken in order at this late hour of art to disembarrass the self-conscious muse and to release her from her chains. This posits an historical impasse (in fact, due not to a poverty but rather to a *superfluity* of possibility), which is closely related to the actual situation in the early years of this century. But this artistic impasse has no real political equivalent, least of all in the affairs of a country as politically immature as the Germany of the Kaiser and, unfortunately, of the Weimar Republic. What Mann surely does tell us here is that psychological wound and cerebral intoxication may be fertile in art, and even ethically justifiable, but that in the political and social sphere they are wholly evil and to be repudiated as such. They are potential sources of strength in art but in politics, only of catastrophe.

The descriptions of the *Apocalyptic Oratorio*—which is clearly intended as directly symbolic of Germany under Hitler—and of the *Lamentation* illustrate the limitations of the suggested parallels between the affairs of art and of politics. The *Apocalyptic Oratorio*, we recall, was written in 'a state of mind which, no longer interested in the psychological, pressed for the objective, for a language that expressed the absolute, the binding and committed . . .' (372), and Zeitblom begins his description of the *Lamentation* with a reiteration of his own lament for the people who had failed to find the appropriate political form for their needs. Now a language which in *politics* 'expresses the absolute, the binding and committed' is not readily related to a technical discipline adopted by an artist. It is what seemed to Mann to be the arbitrariness of the Schoenberg–Leverkühn 12-tone Method that so appalled him and provoked him to the criticism of 'bloodless intellectualism'. But how may one begin to decide whether something which is only, in effect, a catalyst for the artistic imagination, is either 'good' or 'bad'?

Mann's argument could be furthered by asserting that the choice of language and syntax defines a limited expressive world. But even assuming it does, the limitations are surely proper – they are those of whatever moral or aesthetic values are accepted by the artist. The relationship of the language, the system or discipline, to the values accepted is more difficult to establish. What generally matters is, for example, not so much that there is 'one law and all things on earth obey it', but that Schoenberg *believed* that there was. For him, the 12-tone Method was far from being an arbitrary principle – it was a 'natural' law which he had discovered accorded with his irrational beliefs (Sweden borgianism, etc.) It may not be the case that the 12-tone Method is a natural law, but it is enough to ask of Schoenberg (although certainly not of a politician) that he should have adopted it for this reason and not for a purely arbitrary one. It is always possible to invent metaphors, in this instance an artistic one, for sociological and political situations; but to suggest, as Mann would seem to, that serialism exercised as evil an influence on music as a totalitarian regime did on the life and humanity of a nation is hardly satisfactory. In so far as Mann points to music, suggesting that it was symptomatic of the times that there, too, an anarchic excess, which had gone quite outside traditional frameworks, called for and found a rigorous discipline, he is

surely right. But that is rather different, causally at any
rate, from the acceptance of a political discipline which
permitted, or rather demanded, a liberation of the
demonic.

Another serious difficulty is that the reader cannot help
but feel that Leverkühn's music *gains* from his discovery
and adoption of the 12-tone Method, while we know that
it was certainly not Mann's intention to suggest that
totalitarianism was in any way politically desirable; the
Germans had *failed* in their 'last and uttermost attempt
to find the political form suited to their particular needs'.
The explanation here is that Leverkühn's music, a
musique noire, registers its excellence on a negative
scale. The Schoenbergian system is shown as fruitful
within its own terms. It is good of its kind—but for
Mann this was the wrong kind of music! As we have
seen, although Mann had considerable knowledge of it,
he certainly had no special enthusiasm for twentieth-
century music in the Schoenbergian idiom. He may even
have regarded it as in its own way as much an aberration
as the totalitarian principle in politics. There could be no
doubt that total disciplines, the unconditional allegiance
of the element to the larger whole, were capable of
releasing enormous energies. The point was that they
were the wrong, bad, energies, which were better left
untapped.

CHAPTER NINE

Myth, Morality, and the Aesthetic Philosophy

The strictness of the application of the musical discipline in the *Lamentation* is seen as offering at the very end 'a hope beyond hopelessness'. But the motif of hope, of Faust's possible redemption, has always been problematic. Not even Goethe was wholly successful in grafting it onto the traditional legend. It is to the history of that legend that we must now return to see how Mann's own Faust is related to it.

The Faust story is about sinning. It is about one unforgivable sin against which the author, ever concerned for the moral welfare of his readers, continually warns them – the damnation of the hero is an example to all who might feel tempted to follow him. In the enormous numbers of versions of the story (at least fifty have appeared between the second part of Goethe's *Faust* and the present day), the principal variant lies in the authors' widely differing views as to what that one great sin is. The Faust of the first chapbook of 1587 was a magician with small thirst for knowledge or god-like understanding. He employed his special powers mainly in order to play practical jokes and enjoy himself. At the end of the allotted span the devil claimed his soul after punishing the body and leaving the corpse twitching upon a dung heap. The students to whom this Faust made a final

confession were duly impressed. They failed to understand how anyone could have been so reckless as to have
lost body and soul for no more profit than knavery and
for a knowledge which was not even self-knowledge.

Any prospect of Faust's ultimate redemption had to
wait for the Enlightenment; Lessing's Faust fragment of
1759 first sketched this possibility, but it was left to
Goethe to affirm the best hope of Faust's redemption
in the second part of his *Faust* (1832) with its famous
lines:

> Wer immer strebend sich bemüht
> Den können wir erlösen.
>
> (For he whose strivings never cease
> Is ours for his redeeming.)*

Scientific man was now not merely respectable, but had
become the ideal. Goethe the botanist and mineralogist,
Goethe the author of the *Theory of Colours* was bound
to attempt to rescue Faust. Twelve years later in Spain
Zorrilla was to effect a no less sensational and popular
rescue from the flames of hell for Don Juan. Redemption
is looked for in knowledge, truth, and complete experience; damnation is reserved for the stay-at-homes,
the easily satisfied, the unquestioningly faithful and
obedient. The development of the legend thus encom-
passes a new and revolutionary notion: that of the necessity of disobedience as a step towards self-knowledge and
salvation.

A hundred years later Faust is on his way back to
hell—sent there by Thomas Mann for his glorification of
the will and his devaluation of reason and intellect. This
Faust of Mann's is the inverse of Goethe's. It has even

---

* Goethe, *Faust*, Part Two, translated by Philip Wayne, Penguin,
Harmondsworth, 1959, p. 282.

been suggested that the 'good' Goethean Faust is intended to be conspicuous by his absence in a book which assimilates such a very large part of the German tradition of art and thought. The 'ceaseless striving' is there in Leverkühn all right—that is an indispensable Faustian characteristic, for Faust was never known to be damned for his sloth—but it is perverted to become a quality of the will, rather than of the reason and intellect.

Today, the disappearance of faith and the lack of any absolute imperative have left a void at the heart of civilization. As we saw in chapter six (p. 81), it is now Mephisto who supplies the soul and Faust the indifferent omnicompetence. This new Faust is born when man reaches out (particularly through absolute faith in science) to assume powers once considered divine. Mann's Faust reacts, as Nietzsche did, against the absolute claims of reason, which he opposes with an equally absolute claim for the irrational. The devil offers him a boundless inspiration which also supplies the necessary ascendency over awkward little obstacles raised by mind or morality.

Mann quite explicitly took Nietzsche to task for his uncritical celebration of instinctual forces:

> Elementary fairness should counsel us to cherish and protect the feeble little flame of reason, intellect, and justice, and not join sides with power and the instinctual life and riotously whoop it up for negatives, for every sort of criminality. In our contemporary world we have seen the folly of this. Nietzsche did a great deal of mischief by acting as though it were our moral consciousness which, like Mephistopheles, raises an icy, satanic fist [German, = Faust] against life. (LE, 162)

The Faustian pun is clearly intentional, for it defines the enemy against whom the Nietzschean Faust came into

being. Mann even once described Nietzsche in implicitly
Faustian terms:

> ... who in the end was more German than he; who
> served the Germans as still another model for those traits
> which made them a disaster and terror to the world, and
> led them ultimately to ruin themselves: romantic passion,
> the drive to external expansion of the self into space,
> without any fixed object; will which is free because it has
> no goal and aspires to the infinite?   (LE, 175)

Leverkühn is cast by Mann in this mould and it must
certainly have been his hope that the composer's story
would serve as a morality, a lesson in avoidance, just as
the first Faust books had been intended to do.

Mann valued Nietzsche as an extreme and markedly
German contributor to the nineteenth-century revolt
against classical reason. 'This revolt', said Mann, 'has
done its work—or, rather, all that still remains is the
reconstitution of human reason upon a new basis, the
achievement of a concept of humanity of greater pro-
fundity than the complacently shallow view of the
bourgeois age' (LE, 175).

Mann certainly regarded Nietzsche as the later nineteenth century's chief claimant to the gown of Faust. He
described him as a man 'driven to saddle himself with
insights crueller than his temperament can bear, and
who will offer the world the heart-breaking spectacle of
self-crucifixion' (LE, 146). Both Nietzsche and Leverkühn sacrifice themselves in a trial to the uttermost of
their creative powers. Every artist is to some extent
aware of making this sacrifice and we have seen something of what it meant to Mann himself. We may doubt
whether even the tranquillity and ripeness bought of the
passing years ever allowed him to forget his dream of the
'normal', extrovert life as seen in the blond and blue-

eyed Hans Hansen who was unmoved by Schiller's *Don Carlos* but who rode and swam to perfection.

Mann explains how Nietzsche's idea of life as a work of art 'degenerated so brilliantly in his later writings' into that of 'an unreflective culture governed by instinct' (LE, 159)—this being further an exact description of Leverkühn's culture. Nietzsche's idea is ultimately derived from Schopenhauer. Critical though he was of Schopenhauer, it was from him that Nietzsche inherited the notion that the intellect functions merely as a servant of the will, which is seen as the determining factor in the human psyche. Thus, in Leverkühn the will seeks out the blind, inspired, Dionysian state of creative ecstasy which the intellect, after a vigorous initial resistance (in the devil dialogue), then unquestioningly serves. Leverkühn, like Nietzsche, fights against those forces which he holds to be the enemies of life and culture, namely, consciousness and cognition, science, and finally, morality.

Nietzsche himself, particularly the young Nietzsche, was by no means pessimistic or exclusively ruled by apocalyptic visions and prophetic warnings. He greeted a gradual awakening of the Dionysian spirit in the world of 1870. In the depths of the German soul, in German music and philosophy, the rebirth of tragedy was beginning. With Wagner foremost in mind, such at any rate were Nietzsche's hopes. What he did not foresee was the later eruption from these same depths—an eruption not confined to one composer and his initiate followers—which was to lead to the moral and political tragedy which involved a whole world generation. Those responsible for it had preferred to be deaf to the note of hope (which Schopenhauer would have found quite alien) in the motif of redemption through love which overwhelms the

closing bars of Wagner's apocalypse, *his* Götterdäm-
merung. An entire nation of petty-bourgeois boy-scout
Fausts (whom Mann liked to describe as a 'mass-ego' and
whom Nietzsche himself would utterly have disowned)
idiotically obedient to those very nineteenth-century doctrines of the infallibility of the will to which
Nietzsche's soul had already been sacrificed. The lesson
of his self-crucifixion had been ignored and, just as we
learn in *Faustus*, 'A whole host and generation of youth,
receptive, sound to the core, flings itself on the work of
the morbid genius, made genius by disease: admires it,
praises it, exalts it, carries it, assimilates it unto itself . . .'
(242–3).

At this seeming end of German civilization what,
Mann must have thought, could he more conscientiously
do than trace the growth of the malignant strains from
their nineteenth-century breeding ground? How better
to do this than to invoke the Faust legend, that definitive
model of the German's boundless aspiration? This
national legend could be refashioned into a mirror in
which post-war Germany would recognize the greatness
of the culture which had been betrayed. Lest this re-
vitalization of the old story be read as carelessly as
previous texts, Mann would keep the moral well to the
fore in the words of his narrator.

The resonance and generality of the Faust morality are
wide in the extreme. We have already explored some of
the specific cases of its appearance in the novel in such
various fields as religion, philosophy, politics, art and
science. But we must return here to Mann's wide view
of it as a morality for the Germans. He considered it to
be the perfect illustration of those uncomfortable home-
truths which might have been gathered from an intelligent reading of Nietzsche; it is surely not excessive to

hazard that the later Nietzsche intended 'his teaching to
be a warning. . . . He explores this "immoral" way of
life in order to show its consequences, rather than to
make the ideas attractive to us'.*

It was Mann's lament that the Germans' Faustian
tendencies had expressed themselves in the practical
political sphere where it should have been known that
they were bound to have disastrous consequences. The
concerns and ideals of the spirit were not to be confused
with social and ethical reality. For at least twenty years
Mann had warned against this very danger, and we may
therefore read *Doctor Faustus* as his own coda to the
apocalyptic finale of an historical episode whose outcome
he had long foreseen.

*   *   *

Mann saw German culture whole, and in an international perspective. Thus he could criticize (and this
required courage) and see clearly even where he loved.
In his famous lecture of 1933 'Sufferings and Greatness
of Richard Wagner', given in Munich and then in cities
abroad (and whose plain speaking was the immediate
cause of his exile), he had called attention not only to
Wagner's noble qualities but also to the failings which
lent his art an unhealthy nationalistic appeal. Many
passages in the lecture, not surprisingly, tell us as much
about Mann himself as they do about Wagner. Wagner's
Germanness, he says,

> true and mighty as it is, is very modern—it is broken
> down and disintegrating, it is decorative, analytical, intel-
> lectual; and hence its fascination, its inborn capacity for
> cosmopolitan, for world-wide effectiveness. Wagner's art
> is the most sensational self-portrayal and self-critique of

* Paul Roubiczek, *Existentialism: For and Against*, Cambridge
University Press, 1964, p. 42.

the German nature that it is possible to conceive; it is calculated to make Germany interesting to a foreigner even of the meanest intelligence; and passionate preoccupation with it is at the same time passionate preoccupation with the German nature which it so decoratively criticizes and glorifies. In this its nationalism consists; but it is a nationalism so soaked in the currents of European art as to defy all effort to simplify or belittle it.   (E3D, 350)

This assessment applies with greater force to Mann himself than to Wagner: in 1933 Mann was bound to exaggerate the cosmopolitan aspect of Wagner's art. In *Doctor Faustus* he is concerned with the quintessentially German—but this is seen with the eyes of an author who was not bound by this self-preoccupied culture, so that, while still working within it, his writing appeals to a readership not at all limited by national boundaries or language. It is altogether appropriate that this particular German novel should have come to be written thousands of miles away in Los Angeles. Mann's fellow-feeling for Germany and his view of her sufferings and greatness were surely made more intense by the distance of his separation from her, and by the cultural values, so different from her own, in whose midst he found himself having to work. But so complete is his knowledge and understanding that in *Doctor Faustus* he is able to effect the uncharacteristic miracle of a German author delineating the German soul—and to the extent that the novel is autobiographical, that author himself as the German soul's representative—with detached and ironic objectivity.

The Wagner lecture was but one of many opportunities that Mann took to draw the Germans' attention to their tendency to beatify the many embodiments in real-life of Faustian characteristics, their political and social overreachers. Such opportunities included the essay 'Freud and the Future', originally given as a speech in Vienna on May 9th, 1936, in honour of Freud's eightieth birthday, the essays on 'Schopenhauer' and 'Goethe's *Faust*' of 1938, and the revaluation of 'Nietzsche's Philosophy in the Light of Modern History' which too, was actually first given as a speech (in the Library of Congress in 1947), and had been composed in time stolen from work on *Doctor Faustus*. The subject matter of these essays is remarkably continuous with that of the novel. This grew directly out of the writing of all but the last of them, and that is primarily a study in the novel's Nietzschean material.

But while each individual essay concerned itself with a single figure, in the novel Mann crystallized the separate contributions into a representative portrayal of the entire German cultural inheritance. Thus his new Faust is a necessarily fictional figure, unable to be associated too closely with any one of his models.

It is through Mann's critique of these models, particularly as argued in his essays, that we may come to the truest understanding of the morality implicit in *Doctor Faustus*. That morality is in line with the rest of Mann's thought in matters other than political; the innate conservatism of his mind is readily apparent in his tireless interest in critical exposition of the German cultural tradition. It is wholly typical that in 1938, the year of the Munich crisis, he should propose Schopenhauer's philosophy as an anodyne for modern error. He recommends him as a philosopher still to come into his own, as a philosopher of the future:

> I should like to hand on to a world where human feeling is today finding itself in sore straits, the knowledge of this combined melancholy and pride in the human race

L

which make up Schopenhauer's philosophy. . . . We palpably need a corrective to restore the balance, and I think the philosophy I here evoke can do good service. I spoke of Schopenhauer as modern. I might have called him a futurist.   (E3D, 409)

This enthusiasm for Schopenhauer the 'modern' derives from Mann's reading of Hitler's Germany as the incarnation of the philosopher's hypothesis of the will and its characteristics. Schopenhauer urged the necessity of defending ourselves against the unruly drives of the will (which, it will be remembered, Mann saw as a forerunner of Freud's id) by subjecting it to mind and reason. So for Leverkühn to place his outstanding intellect at the disposal of his will, rather than employ it against it, as Schopenhauer had taught, was the deadliest betrayal of his own humanity. Leverkühn is representative of those qualities of the will described by Mann in the Schopenhauer essay, where he battles to tell us that the philosopher's

> interpretation of the world by the concept of the will, his insight into the overweening power of instinct and the derogation of the one-time godlike reason, mind and intellect to a mere tool with which to achieve security— all this is anti-classic and in its essence inhumane.   (E3D, 409)

Furthermore, Mann argued that Schopenhauer's philosophic and psychological preoccupation with the will necessarily makes him a pessimist:

> Will, as the opposite pole of passive satisfaction, is naturally a fundamental unhappiness, it is unrest, a striving for *something*—it is want, craving, avidity, demand, suffering; and a world of will can be nothing else but a world of suffering.   (E3D, 381)

Zeitblom writes of the Christlike suffering seen on Leverkühn's face in his latter years, and of his deliber-

ately seeking out suffering so as to sacrifice himself upon
its altar, as Nietzsche had done. A few pages further on in
the essay, it is no surprise to find Mann quoting the young
Nietzsche:

> 'I found pleasurable in Wagner what I do in Schopen-
> hauer: the ethical air, the Faustian flavour, Cross, Death,
> and Grave.' It is, [Mann comments] the prevailing intel-
> lectual atmosphere of the second half of the nineteenth
> century—the air of youth and home for those of us past
> sixty.   (E3D, 394)

And he goes straight on to say how music 'belongs to this
ethical-pessimistic atmosphere'. He stresses Schopenhauer's musicality and the high place he ascribed to this
art because music was 'the image of the will itself' and
thus depicted 'the metaphysical, to all appearance the
thing itself'.

We can summarize the Schopenhauerian contribution
to *Doctor Faustus* as first, the idea of music as representing the will, and second, the idea that Faust's great sin
is to allow intellect to be subject to will, rather than to
use it in creative opposition to will. Where might lie the
best hope of redemption? It is to Goethe that Mann turns
for enlightenment, for it is in Goethe's spirit that he
speaks of Schopenhauer's

> doctrine of redemption which he has built into, which
> emerges from, his philosophy of the will . . . there *is*
> release from miseries and mistakes, from the errors and
> penalties of this life. This gift is laid in the hand of the
> human being, the highest and most developed objecti-
> fication of the will, and accordingly the most richly
> capable of suffering . . . the core of our being, the will,
> which is the will to live, remains entirely unassailed, and
> can, *if it continues to affirm itself*, seek out fresh avenues
> of approach to life.   (E3D, 383)

The italics are Mann's own and draw attention to a doubtless intended reference to the Goethean Faust, whose ceaseless striving wins him the promise of redemption—does this not relate closely to the concept of the will, bent for once not on annihilation, but on self-affirmation? Mann draws a direct comparison between Schopenhauer and Goethe in order to give more point to his critique of the former:

> . . . suppose he [Schopenhauer] had understood that genius does not at all consist in sensuality put out of action and will unhinged, that art is not mere objectification of both spheres, immensely heightening to life and more fascinating than either can be by itself! . . . Goethe's interpretation and experience differed from the pessimist's; it was happier, healthier, more blithely classical, less pathologic (I use the word in an intellectual, unclinical sense)—less romantic, shall I say?   (E3D, 406)

It was these very same Goethean ideas which so surprised his friends when Leverkühn advanced them in discussion. In words that they found quite uncharacteristic of the composer, he looked forward to the redemption of art from its 'pompous isolation' and from undue self-seriousness, into something gayer, less romantic, more *naiv*:

'The whole temper of art, believe me, will change', Leverkühn tells his friends, '. . . Much melancholy ambition will fall away from her, and a new innocence, yes, harmlessness will be hers. . . . We can only with difficulty imagine such a thing: an art without anguish, psychologically healthy, not solemn, unsadly confiding, an art *per Du* with humanity' (322). It is significant that Mann should give these words (which express his own personal ideas) to Leverkühn when he at last begins to regret his pact and to look for redemption now not

through the devil, but *from* him and his demonic art. To
Mann, hope for such redemption was to be sought in the
philosophy of Goethe rather than in that of Schopenhauer,
whatever other lessons Schopenhauer's thought might
contain. And it was to Goethe that Mann himself looked to
temper what might otherwise have been a fatal affinity for
'the Faustian flavour, Cross, Death, and Grave' which he
too so enjoyed in Schopenhauer, Wagner and Nietzsche.

Mann must often have felt that that affinity was
associated with his own Faustian streak, and we must
now turn to the confessional burden borne by his novel.
This is rooted in his own sense of involvement in a life-
long Faustian pact which had made him the writer that he
was. There were great achievements to look back upon, but
they had been bought at a price. When he came to write
Doctor Faustus the time was ripe to acknowledge it.

Just how closely Mann identified himself with the
German intellectual tradition will be apparent. It is
scarcely possible to over-emphasize this identification,
which involves a highly developed mythical awareness.
His preoccupations with myth are quite explicit in
his essay 'Freud and the Future' where they were
directly occasioned by his work on the Joseph novels, but
they are characteristic and are no less evident in his
response to the Faust story. He refers to an essay*
by an unnamed Viennese scholar of the Freudian school:

> to my delight, but scarcely to my surprise, he begins to
> cite from *Joseph*, the fundamental motif of which he says
> is precisely this idea of the 'lived life', life as succession,
> as a moving in others' steps, as identification—such as
> Joseph's teacher, Eliezer, practises with droll solemnity.

* This is 'Zur Psychologie der älteren Biographik' by Ernst Kris,
first published in *Imago*, XXI, 1935, and translated as 'The Image
of the Artist' in the author's *Psychoanalytic Explorations in Art*,
George Allen & Unwin, London, 1953.

For in him time is cancelled and all the Eliezers of the past gather to shape the Eliezer of the present, so that he speaks in the first person of that Eliezer who was Abram's servant, though he was far from being the same man. (E3D, 421–2)

The scholar's essay, Mann continues, 'makes it clear that the typical is actually the mythical, and that one may as well say "lived myth" as "lived life". But the mythus as lived is the epic idea embodied in my novel . . .'. With obvious approval, Mann quotes Ortega y Gasset's aphorism that the man of antiquity, before he did anything, took a step backwards, like the bullfighter who leaps back to deliver the mortal thrust:

He searched the past for a pattern into which he might slip as into a diving bell, and being thus at once disguised and protected might rush upon his present problem. Thus his life was in a sense a reanimation, an archaizing attitude. But it is just this life as reanimation that is the life as myth. (E3D, 424)

Doctor Faustus, too, is certainly a work which largely refers to and appeals to the myth and which 'only through it, through reference to the past, could . . . approve itself as genuine and significant' (E3D, 424). More tellingly still Mann describes how

the *imitatio* Goethe, with its Werther and Wilhelm Meister stages, its old-age period of *Faust* and *Diwan*, can still shape and mythically mould the life of an artist—rising out of his unconscious, yet playing over—as is the artist's way—into a smiling, childlike, and profound awareness. (E3D, 426)

This, as we have seen, was Mann's ideal—although he was to approach it far more nearly in *Felix Krull* than in the mythopoeic *Doctor Faustus*.

What Mann has to say about the artist's sense of a

past reborn in himself is obviously of personal significance. It must have seemed likely to him that Faustus would be his last major work, and we are surely right to see in his choice of the old Faust story a valedictory confession that this was the mythic role with which he most closely identified. *Doctor Faustus*, as we recall, was 'confession and sacrifice through and through and hence would not be bound by considerations of mere discretion' (GN, 73).

How then did Mann see himself as Faust and what did he consider his pact, his sacrifice for the sake of winning special powers, to have been? It would seem that he never ceased to regard himself, just as Tonio Kröger did, as

> a bourgeois who strayed off into art, a bohemian who feels nostalgic yearnings for respectability, an artist with a bad conscience. For surely it is my *bourgeois* conscience makes me see in the artist life, in all irregularity and all genius, something profoundly disreputable . . .   (SOL1, 208)

His pact had been required in order to realize his literary ambitions, to satisfy the determination of the creative intellect rather than yield to the melancholy preference of the will. Yet was Mann really the bourgeois that he imagined? Maybe it *was* his bourgeois conscience which saw something disreputable in the artist life, but it was the true artist in him which sharpened his awareness of the dark forces beneath the surface. For the bourgeois is not self-aware and Mann's highly intelligent self-awareness, and his inability to avoid the artist's demonic dialogue with himself, place him beyond the bourgeois pale. His longing for bourgeois normality was the temptation to damning ease and contentment in one in whom the creative impulse is already firmly rooted. A longing for such 'normality' is the principal enemy of that 'ceaseless

striving' whereby he who is called to it may alone hope
for fulfilment and redemption. It is surely significant
that Leverkühn's dialogue with his devil should have
taken place in Italy in the self-same place (Palestrina)
where Mann and his brother Heinrich stayed for a
summer spell in the 1890s. It was in Palestrina that
Buddenbrooks was begun. The misfit bourgeois with the
strongly developed Faustian leaning had known that he
had it in him to accomplish much as a writer. Looking
back over his life from the time of writing *Faustus*,
there could be no doubt that he had succeeded, even if
he had had to fight down the Hans Hansen in him so
that the Tonio Kröger might flourish.

But Mann was caught in much more than a straightforward 'art or life' dilemma. He discovered that it was
impossible to wish away his sensibility, or to transform
his creative drive into an uncomplicated enjoyment of the
life around him. In Leverkühn we are shown a deliberately cool and objective philosophy as a condition for
artistic production. His was an inhumanity in life for the
sake of an enhanced humanity in his art. This is seen in
extreme form in Leverkühn, but Mann too made some
sacrifice to this effect. In *Tonio Kröger*, it was he himself
who hoped that 'if anything is capable of making a poet
(*Dichter*) of a literary man, it is my bourgeois love of the
human, the living and usual. It is the source of all
warmth, goodness, and humour; I even almost think it is
itself that love of which it stands written that one may
speak with the tongues of men and angels and yet
having it not is as sounding brass and tinkling cymbals'
(SOL1, 208–9). We may also recall Hans Castorp's vision
of the saving grace of that love which comes to him while
semi-conscious and lost out in the snows, the love which
marks the turning point of his development in the Bil-

dungsroman *The Magic Mountain*. Mann contrasts this love with its absence in 'those proud, cold beings who adventure upon the paths of great and demonic beauty and despise "mankind" '. The truth was that, however much he may have wished to affirm his love for 'the human, the living and the usual', and for 'the fair and living, the happy, lovely and commonplace', it was his *interest** in weakness, disease and decadence which afforded the greater stimulus to art. With the special exception of the Joseph novels, Mann's fiction is more notable for its von Aschenbachs and Leverkühns than for its Hans Hansens. Against his better judgement, his art had been more closely associated with the pathology of life than with a celebration of its finer qualities. The artist had been true to his experience, which for him had had to be bad. He had wanted to write a Ninth Symphony, but had ended up by unwriting it, so that all he could offer in *Doctor Faustus* was a lament and confession that it had had to be so.

Mann was the Faustian intellectual par excellence, always a little sick from excess of knowledge and deficiency of belief. Music, in particular, helped to fill out that emotional dimension which the intellectual to some extent lacked. As a strong and formidably intelligent personality, Mann was in no danger of getting life so confused with art as did the twins in *The Blood of the Walsungs* after they had heard *Die Walküre*, but he might well have endorsed Siegmund Aarenhold's reflection: '. . . his life, so full of words, so void of acts, so full of cleverness, so empty of emotion—and he felt again the burning, the drawing anguish which yet was sweet

---

* Cf. Leverkühn's previously quoted reply to Zeitblom's enquiry as to whether he knows a stronger emotion than love, 'Yes, interest' (69).

–whither, and to what end? Creation? Experience? Passion?' (SOL1, 352). Leverkühn's indifferent omnicompetence lacks but one thing, a soul, and it is this, together with an adequate measure of inspirational ecstasy, which the devil undertakes to provide–as he was to a lesser extent called upon to supply in Mann's own life. Disease spurs Leverkühn on to composition; music–and ideas aspiring to its condition–were a scarcely less powerful stimulant for Mann's own creative imagination. Among those who could supply his favourite stimulants were Schopenhauer, Wagner and Nietzsche: it was nearly always Wagner, seldom the clear, cool draught of Bach. He was himself, then, intimately aware of the seductions awaiting those susceptible to the Klingsor spells of nineteenth-century art and thought.

Mann's pact had also opened up an embarrassing gulf between the aesthetic philosophy of the creative writer and the responsibility felt by the good citizen to declare his ethical values. The language of his aesthetic philosophy was irony. This irony identifies him as one of Schiller's *sentimentalische Dichter* who are aware of an unbridgeable gulf between themselves and the world around them. However much Mann regretted it–and his regret is clear enough from his longing for a new art that would once again be *per Du* with humanity–the alienation was the reality. Commitment and direct statement are the privilege of the *naiv*, of those who believe. And if one may not believe, if one's attitude should happen to be the Faustian one of a passion for truth and of no belief in it (as Mann's certainly was *), then what remains

---

* We may cite two characteristic examples of Mann's own amoral trait of passion unsupported by belief. Of his reading of Nietzsche he once wrote:

I took nothing literally; I *believed* him hardly at all; and this

open to one is to know what can be known, and to place one's faith in that, and to do what can be done. The process is self-vindicating, for the more one knows, the less one feels one needs to believe. Thus there is knowledge and observation, transformed by the imagination and expressed in a language of high ironic artistry which protects the artist from any ethical obligation other than that of commitment to the aesthetic philosophy. This commitment had enabled Mann to take the game a little further in a late and exceptionally critical period for art. It was with good reason that he was known by his family as 'Der Zauberer'.

'With deep concern I asked myself what strain and effort, intellectual tricks, by-ways, and ironies would be necessary to save it, to reconquer it and to arrive at a work which as a travesty of innocence confessed to the state of knowledge from which it was to be won!' (181). Zeitblom's words about the future of art are to be read as Mann's own. They acknowledge his exploitation of irony to help him penetrate beyond introspective self-consciousness in order to establish an art which would be Aristotelian 'play for the sake of seriousness'. Thus he hoped to assert the vitality of an art at once aesthetic and

---

precisely made my love for him a passion on two planes—gave it, in other words, its depth.   (SML, 23)

And of his reading of Schopenhauer:

I am not much disturbed by the question of the *truth* of Schopenhauer's interpretations . . .   (E3D, 403)

Despite Mann's grateful acknowledgement to Schopenhauer for his revelation that pessimism and humanism in no wise exclude the other and 'that in order to be a humanist one does not need to be a rhetorical flatterer of humanity', this does read a little oddly against his recommendation of the 'good service' yet to be done by Schopenhauer's philosophy.

human by his refusal to make any claims for it as knowledge.

Although this strategy was abundantly justified by result, there are reservations which should be made about Mann's ironic stance, particularly when he adopted it because he was unable to make up his mind about this or that. Thus Mann, in the person of Zeitblom, is usually ready to distrust what, in that of Leverkühn, he appears to propose. Kierkegaard, Erich Heller reminds us (HIG, 209), once defined irony as the incognito of the moralist, because his manner of existing inwardly cannot be expressed in terms of the world. But is it not reasonable that we should expect the would-be moralist to be able to be resolved about his material? Should not his values be apparent in his irony? And if, at a certain time, it is impossible for him to solve a moral dilemma, should it not be placed in as clear cut a form as possible before the reader, so that he can attempt to solve it as he may? Yet Mann seems to have preferred to preserve areas of indecision; where Zeitblom is uncertain as to what is going on, this generally reflects Mann's own uncertainty. 'Maybe it is good to be resolute', he once said, 'but the really fruitful principle, the principle of art, is . . . reserve', namely, 'that irony which plays subtly and undecidedly . . . among the opposites, and is in no great hurry to join issue . . .' (E3D, 173). It is therefore no wonder that the ambivalent and equivocal are central topics in the work of a writer so committed to strategic non-committal.

There is no doubt that his ambivalence, his essentially aesthetic rather than ethical temperament, was a source of deep disturbance to Mann. Accounting it part and parcel of the artist's 'necessary' sickness, of the price to be paid for the privilege of the creative life, he learned

to live with it. Even as early as 1917 he could write thus
of the many people who had said that his books had
'helped them to live':

> I had too many problems with myself to imagine con-
> ceitedly that I would be able to help others. And yet I
> have helped others, and quite obviously *many* others, to
> live! I was not being social, not political; I did not pose
> with my right hand on my heart and my left in the air,
> reciting the *Contrat social*. And therefore I was no
> 'fighter', but an 'aesthete'. And still I helped people to
> live. That much I may tell myself at forty, and if I
> accomplish no more to the day of my death, I shall also
> be able to say it still in death. *

Yet in *Doctor Faustus* Mann was able to effect a limited
resolution of the competing claims of the ethical need to
declare his absolute opposition to National Socialism, and
of the artist's aesthetic need for free play with his
material. No longer content to reserve his opinions for
speeches, broadcasts, and private communications, he
comes out from time to time in *Faustus*. From behind the
ironic mask, and speaks up as a vigilant referee of the
rights and wrongs of his story. His own voice is heard
most obviously in Zeitblom's political tirades, but often
also in the discussions in which his characters take part.

Perhaps we should see Mann's failure to achieve an
integrated ironic whole in this novel as a confirmation of
the irreconcilable nature of the claims of the spirit and
those of social and political reality. He certainly knew
that they *were* competing claims. He took Nietzsche to
task for presenting life *or* morality as the fundamental
conflict rather than the ethical/aesthetic dilemma felt by
Kierkegaard, which was more in accordance with his
own experience. 'Ethics is the prop of life', said Mann,

---

* *Letters to Paul Amann*, pp. 87–8.

'and the moral man a true citizen of life's realm – perhaps a somewhat boring fellow, but highly useful. The real dichotomy lies between ethics and aesthetics' (LE, 162).

For all this ethical plain speaking, Mann had no intention of being over apologetic about the seriousness and validity of the aesthetic game itself. Leverkühn assures Zeitblom that at bottom there is only one problem in the world: 'How does one break through? How does one get into the open? How does one burst the cocoon and become a butterfly?' Leverkühn continues by praising the treatment of the same theme in Kleist's *Über das Marionettentheater*, with the single reservation that 'it is talking only about the aesthetic, charm, and free grace, which are actually reserved to the automaton and the god' (308). Mann pleads the common concerns of art and ethics by having Zeitblom interject: 'But do not say it is speaking only of aesthetics, do not say *only*! One does wrong to see in aesthetics a separate and narrow field of the humane.' As illustration of the dialogue between artistic and ethical values in *Doctor Faustus*, we have already cited the juxtaposition of the table-talk of the politically irresponsible Kridwiss group with the description of the demonically intellectual *Apocalyptic Oratorio*.

It is a major contribution of Mann's novel that it sidesteps no issues in the ethical/aesthetic argument and arrives at no easy solution. It asserts the persistence of the conflicting demands of the two claims. For how are we to reconcile the two parts of Zeitblom's double-role? Is it possible to reconcile the Zeitblom whose denunciations of Germany might have been lifted straight from Mann's political broadcasts, with the ironic Zeitblom, the chronicler of Leverkühn's life and times? How could Mann allow himself those so thinly disguised outbursts

of personal response in a novel? This response was something which he had formerly been to some pains to keep
out of his fiction. We must surely conclude that in this
one novel the compromising of the aesthetic mode is
highly deliberate. The Nazi catastrophe had convinced
Mann that the moral of the Faust story should never for
a minute be forgotten. *Doctor Faustus* is not so much an
attempt to resolve the dilemma of the politically responsible artist, as to allow full statement of it.

At the last we cannot help but return to praise the
manifold subleties of Mann's irony. Learned by him from
Schopenhauer and Nietzsche, it becomes the means of
his deliverance from the thrall of pessimism, self-consciousness and excess of knowledge. He once wrote of
Nietzsche:

> . . . something spurious, irresponsible, unreliable, and
> passionately frivolous existed within these philosophical
> effusions. That something was an element of deepest
> irony which thwarts the understanding of the simpler
> reader . . . anyone who takes Nietzsche 'as he is', who
> believes him and takes him at his word, is lost. (LE,
> 173)

This applies equally to himself. What Schopenhauer had
preached in theory, and what had kept Nietzsche's madness at bay, serving for him as a necessarily 'musical'
medium for ideas bearing too high a charge to allow of
their plain statement, is in Mann turned coolly and consciously to creative purpose. Mann's irony transcends not
only his material (the German tradition itself) but is
self-transcending.

That this is so is a hazard to the critic. He is continually exposed to the charge that any attempt to penetrate the irony is bound to be speculation or a misleading
simplification. One may certainly insist that whatever

else it may or may not be about, this novel stands against that 'simplification of the emotions' which, Mann pointed out, Hitler had been so successful in imposing (GN, 131). *Doctor Faustus* is a testament to the diversity and complexity of life. Its inbuilt elusiveness (which makes one so reluctant to formulate, let alone to comment on, Mann's 'meaning') is all of a piece with its musical theme; for, just as with a musical work, although one can discuss its technical aspect perfectly properly, and one can discuss the idea of the whole, its life and substance guard their secret closely. We may discuss the irony, the *idea* of the book and of its themes and characters, but only cautiously these things themselves. Mann, the student of Schopenhauer, used his art not least to set a beguiling maze around *das Ding an sich*.

In his essay on the philosopher, Mann wrote of Schopenhauer's Apollo, 'who shoots his arrow from afar', as characterization of

> a god of distance, of space, not of pathos and pathology or involvement, a god not of suffering but of freedom. He is an objective god, the god of irony. In irony, then, as Schopenhauer saw it, in creative objectivity, knowledge was freed from its bondage to will, and the attention was no longer blurred by any motive.   (E3D, 385)

This led Mann directly to that detached, aesthetic philosophy which was more appropriate to the artist than to the responsible citizen. But he learned one vital thing here from Nietzsche, namely that the artist and the citizen should hold each other in proper respect. He thus took care in *Doctor Faustus* to preserve and to assert the persistence of the conflict between aesthetic and ethical demands. Nietzsche held that the aesthetic, or perhaps we should say *his* aesthetic, *contained* the moral. He regarded 'morality' as antagonistic to life, that is, the dance of Dionysian life which is its own aesthetic justification. Over this point Mann rounded firmly on Nietzsche, arguing that life and morality are not antagonists and that they belong together, the real dichotomy being that between ethics and aesthetics. The defence of instinct against reason and consciousness, Mann believed, was a corrective needed at a specific moment:

> but permanently, eternally necessary is the correction of life by mind—or by morality, if you will. . . . In the final analysis aestheticism, under whose banner freethinkers turned against bourgeois morality, itself belonged to the bourgeois age. And to go beyond this age means to step out of an aesthetic era into a moral and social one.   (LE, 176)

These are surely the words of one whose creativity lay in aesthetic rather than in moral and social matters. For this view is a conventional wisdom. It tells us less about either life or art than may be learnt from those works in which the free play of Mann's artistic imagination is more readily apparent. The intransigence of the ethical/ aesthetic dilemma was no mean source of his strength, and that dilemma is perhaps more fundamental than even he knew. It is a wound which we need to keep open, for it would seem to close only in response to remedies more damaging than itself.

M

Appendix

The exchange of letters between Schoenberg and Mann in *The Saturday Review of Literature*, January 1st, 1949.

'Doctor Faustus' Schoenberg?

Sir: In his novel *Doctor Faustus* [SRL Oct. 30] Thomas Mann has taken advantage of my literary property. He has produced a fictitious composer as the hero of his book; and in order to lend him qualities a hero needs to arouse people's interest, he made him the creator of what one erroneously calls my 'system of twelve tones', which I call 'method of composing with twelve tones'.

He did this without my permission and even without my knowledge. In other words, he borrowed it in the absence of the proprietor. The supposition of one reviewer, that he obtained information about his technique from Bruno Walter and Stravinsky, is probably wrong; because Walter does not know anything of composition with twelve tones, and Stravinsky does not take any interest in it.

The informer was Mr. Wiesengrund-Adorno, a former pupil of my late friend Alban Berg. Mr. Adorno is very well acquainted with all the extrinsic details of this technique and thus was capable of giving Mr. Mann quite an accurate account of what a layman – the author – needs to tell another layman – the reader – to make him believe that he understands what it is about. But still, this was my property and nobody else's.

I learned about this abuse by chance: I received a magazine, containing a review of 'Doctor Faustus', wherein the twelve-notes composition was mentioned.

Thereafter, Mrs. Alma Mahler-Werfel told me that she had read the book and was very upset about his using my 'theory', without naming me as author, while he includes many living persons—Walter, Klemperer, etc., not as fictitious, but as real people. I have still not read the book itself, though in the meantime Mann had sent me a German copy, with a handwritten dedication, 'To A. Schoenberg, dem Eigentlichen [the real one].' As one need not tell me that I am an 'Eigentlichen', a real one, it was clear that he wanted to tell me that his Leverkuehn is an impersonation of myself.

Leverkuehn is depicted, from beginning to end, as a lunatic. I am now seventy-four and I am not yet insane, and I have never acquired the disease from which this insanity stems. I consider this an insult, and I might have to draw consequences.

When Mrs. Mahler-Werfel discovered this misuse of my property, she told Mann that this was my theory, whereupon he said: 'Oh, does one notice that? Then perhaps Mr. Schoenberg will be angry!' This proves that he was conscious of his guilt, and knew it was a violation of an author's right.

It was very difficult for Mrs. Mahler-Werfel to convince him that he must do something to correct this wrong.

Finally I sent him a letter and showed him the possible consequences of ascribing my creation to another person which, in spite of being fictitious, is represented like a living man, whose biography is told by his friend Serenus Zeitblom.

One knows the superficiality and monomania of some historians who ignore facts if they do not fit in their hypotheses. Thus I quoted from an encyclopedia of the year 2060, a little article in which my theory was attributed to Thomas Mann, because of his Leverkuehn.

Much pressure by Mrs. Mahler-Werfel had still to be exerted to make Mann promise that every forthcoming copy of 'Doctor Faustus' will carry a note giving me credit for the twelve-notes composition. I was satisfied by this promise, because I wanted to be noble to a man who was awarded the Nobel Prize.

But Mr. Mann was not as generous as I, who had given him good chance to free himself from the ugly aspect of a pirate. He gave an explanation: a few lines which he hid at the end of the book on a place on a page where no one ever would see it. Besides, he added a new crime to his first, in the attempt to belittle me: He calls me 'a [a!] *contemporary* composer and theoretician.' Of course, in two or three decades, one will know which of the two was the other's contemporary.

ARNOLD SCHOENBERG

Los Angeles, Calif.

Sir: . . . Arnold Schoenberg's letter both astonished and grieved me. Our personal correspondence on this matter had been of a thoroughly friendly character in all its phases. Not so long ago, when I sent him the English edition of 'Doctor Faustus' with my appended statement, the maestro thanked me cordially with an air of complete satisfaction, so that I was led to believe that the 'Leverkuehn Case' was settled and disposed of. Now I regret to learn that it not only continues to annoy him but actually irritates him increasingly, although he still has not read the book.

If his acquaintance with the book were not based exclusively on the gossip of meddling scandal mongers, he would know that my efforts to give the central figure of the novel 'qualities a hero needs to arouse people's

interest' were neither limited to the transfer of Schoenberg's 'method of composing with twelve tones', nor was
this characteristic the most important one. Quaintly
enough, he calls this technique his 'literary property',
though actually it should be called a musical system that
has long since become a part of our cultural pattern, used
by countless composers throughout the world, all of
whom have tacitly purloined it from its originator. The
universal dissemination and the wide employment of
this technique are the very factors underlying the basic
error of which I accuse myself. I sincerely believed that
every child in our cultural area [sic] must at one time or
another have heard about the twelve-tone system and its
initiator, and that no one on earth, having read my
novel, could possibly imagine that I was its inventor or
was trying to pose as such. This opinion of mine, I must
say, was confirmed by many Swiss, German, Swedish,
and, more recently, French reviews of the book, in
which Schoenberg's name was quite casually mentioned.
It was he himself who enlightened me with respect to
my error. Serious misunderstandings, he informed me,
would result from my book, unless I did something about
it. Everybody except him, he said, kept receiving credit
for his creation, and, if he knew anything about the
breed of musicologists, they would attribute his theory
to me a hundred years from now because I had developed it in my novel. His contemporaries, he added,
were withholding so much from him that he had, at
least, to guard his name and fame for posterity.

His concluding word moved me, no matter how absurd
his apprehension seemed. It is quite untrue that it required 'much pressure' to induce me to give him due
credit. As soon as I understood his concern I gave instruc-
tions to include in all translations, as well as in the

German original, the appended statement which now appears in the English edition of 'Doctor Faustus'. It was intended as a bit of instruction to the uninformed, and I worded it as objectively as possible. 'Take note,' it says in effect, 'there is a composer and music philosopher living among us, whose name is Arnold Schoenberg; he, and not the hero of my novel, is the one who, in reality, thought out the twelve-tone composition method.' The statement does not raise the question who is whose contemporary. If Schoenberg wishes, we shall, all of us, consider it our greatest and proudest claim to be his contemporaries.

As soon as I had received the first copies of the German edition I sent him one with the inscription; 'Dem Eigentlichen ["To the real one"]'. It meant: 'Not Leverkuehn is the hero of this musical era; you are its hero.' It was a bow, a compliment. I have always addressed Arnold Schoenberg, the uncompromising and bold artist, with the utmost respect, in personal contact as well as in my letters, and I shall continue to do so.

The idea that Adrian Leverkuehn is Schoenberg, that the figure is a portrait of him, is so utterly absurd that I scarcely know what to say about it. There is no point of contact, not a shade of similarity, between the origin, the traditions, the character, and the fate of my musician, on the one hand, and the existence of Schoenberg, on the other. 'Doctor Faustus' has been called a Nietzsche-novel and, indeed, the book, which for good reasons avoids mention of Nietzsche's name, contains many references to his intellectual tragedy, even direct quotations from the history of his illness. It has also been said that I bisected myself in the novel, and that the narrator and the hero each embraced a part of me. That, also, contains an element of truth—although I, too, do not suffer from paralysis. But it has not occurred to anyone to speak of a Schoenberg-novel.

Instead of accepting my book with a satisfied smile as a piece of contemporary literature that testifies to his tremendous influence upon the musical culture of the era, Schoenberg regards it as an act of rape and insult. It is a sad spectacle to see a man of great worth, whose all-too-understandable hypersensitivity grows out of a life suspended between glorification and neglect, almost wilfully yield to delusions of persecution and of being robbed, and involve himself in rancorous bickering. It is my sincere hope and wish that he may rise above bitterness and suspicion and that he may find peace in the assurance of his greatness and glory!

THOMAS MANN

Pacific Palisades, Calif.

Bibliography

This bibliography is by no means comprehensive, its first purpose being to acknowledge my sources. It contains many more items than those specifically referred to in the text, and includes a selection of the better studies available in English. The place of publication, unless given otherwise, is London. The standard bibliographies listed will guide the reader into the remotest corners of the vast, and ever expanding, literature on Thomas Mann.

(1) MANN'S WORKS IN ENGLISH TRANSLATION, AND IN GERMAN

Unless otherwise indicated, the English translations of Mann's works are by Mrs H. T. Lowe-Porter and are published by Secker and Warburg, London, and Alfred A. Knopf, New York. Where the edition cited is not the first English edition, the date of the latter is given in brackets. I have occasionally revised the translation in quoting. References to *Doctor Faustus*, 1949, are given thus (243). References to several other works are given in abbreviated forms, thus (GN, 175).

BB	*Buddenbrooks* (1924), 1930.
MM	*The Magic Mountain* (1927), 1946.
E3D	*Essays of Three Decades*, 1947.
HS	*The Holy Sinner*, 1952.
LE	*Last Essays*, translated by Richard and Clara Winston, and Tania and James Stern, 1959.
SOL (1 & 2)	*Stories of a Lifetime*, Two Vols., Heinemann (Mercury Books), London, 1961.
SML	*A Sketch of My Life*, 1961.
GN	*The Genesis of a Novel*, translated by Richard and Clara Winston, 1961.
TMA	*Thomas Mann's Addresses*, Washington: Library of Congress, 1963.

Letters to Paul Amann, translated by Richard and Clara Winston, and edited by Herbert Wegener, 1961.

Letters of Thomas Mann, selected and translated from the three volume S. Fischer edition (see below), with some additional letters, by Richard and Clara Winston, Two Vols., 1970.

*   *   *

Unless otherwise indicated, publishers of Mann's works in German are the S. Fischer Verlag (Berlin and Frankfurt) which between 1936 and 1949 became the Bermann-Fischer Verlag (Vienna, Stockholm and Amsterdam).

Gesammelte Werke in zwölf Bänden, edited by Hans Bürgin, Frankfurt, 1960. *Doktor Faustus* is Volume VI. This is the most complete edition so far available. The other standard editions are:

Stockholmer Gesamtausgabe, Stockholm-Amsterdam-Vienna, 1938–49, and Frankfurt, 1950–58.

Gesammelte Werke in zwölf Bänden, East Berlin: Aufbau Verlag, 1955. (Supposedly on sale only in the German Democratic Republic, but in fact often available elsewhere.)

Briefe 1889–1936, edited by Erika Mann, Frankfurt, 1961.

Briefe 1937–1947, edited by Erika Mann, Frankfurt, 1963.

Briefe 1948–1955 und Nachlese, edited by Erika Mann, Frankfurt, 1965.

Briefe an Paul Amann 1915–1952, edited by Herbert Wegener, Lübeck: Schmidt-Römhild, 1959.

Thomas Mann an Ernst Bertram. Briefe aus den Jahren 1910–1955, edited by Inge Jens, Pfullingen: Neske, 1960.

Mann, Thomas und Karl Kerényi. *Gespräch in Briefen*, Zürich: Rhein Verlag, 1960.

Mann, Thomas und Robert Faesi. *Briefwechsel*, Zürich: Atlantis Verlag, 1962.

Hermann Hesse–Thomas Mann: Briefwechsel, edited by Anni Carlsson, Frankfurt: Suhrkamp, 1968.

Thomas Mann–Heinrich Mann: Briefwechsel, edited by Hans Wysling, Frankfurt, 1969.

Wagner und unsere Zeit, edited by Erika Mann, Frankfurt, 1963. A convenient collection of Mann's most important essays and writings (1902–51) on Wagner.

(2) Secondary literature on Mann

GBF Bergsten, Gunilla. *Thomas Mann's 'Doctor Faustus': the Sources and Structure of the Novel*. Translated by Krishna Winston. University of Chicago Press, 1969.

Bürgin, Hans. *Das Werk Thomas Manns, eine Bibliographie*. Frankfurt, 1959.

Bürgin, Hans, and Mayer, Hans-Otto. *Thomas Mann: A Chronicle of His Life*. A revised version of the German original (Frankfurt, 1965) translated by Eugene Dobson. Alabama University Press, 1969. In the absence of a standard biography, this detailed chronology of Mann's life and work is the most useful record available.

Dierks, Manfred. *Studien zu Mythos und Psychologie bei Thomas Mann*. Berne, 1972. The second volume in the important series of 'Thomas-Mann-Studien', edited by the Thomas Mann Archive in Zurich. See also below under Scherrer, Paul, and Wysling, Hans.

Hatfield, Henry. *Thomas Mann*. Revised paperback edition. Connecticut, 1962.

HIG Heller, Erich. *Thomas Mann The Ironic German*. Meridian paperback book. Cleveland, 1961. The earlier English edition, under a slightly different title, was published by Secker and Warburg, 1958.

Holthusen, Hans Egon. *Die Welt ohne Transzendenz: eine Studie zu Thomas Manns 'Dr. Faustus' und seinen Nebenschriften*. Hamburg, 1949.

Jonas, Klaus W. *Die Thomas-Mann-Literatur: Bibliographie der Kritik 1896–1955*. Berlin, 1972.

Jonas, Klaus W., and Ilsedore B. *Fifty Years of Thomas Mann Studies*. University of Minnesota Press, 1955. *Thomas Mann Studies, Volume 2*. University of Pennsylvania Press, 1967. Between them, these two books mention more than 7,000 items.

Kahler, Erich. *The Orbit of Thomas Mann*. Princeton University Press, 1969.

Kaufmann, Fritz. *Thomas Mann: the World as Will and Representation*. Boston, 1957.

Lindsay, J. M. *Thomas Mann*. Oxford: Blackwell, 1954.

Lukács, Georg. *Essays on Thomas Mann*. Translated by Stanley Mitchell. Merlin Press, 1964.

Mann, Erika. *The Last Year*. Translated by Richard Graves. Secker and Warburg, 1958.

Mann, Victor. *Wir waren fünf: Bildnis der Familie Mann*. Konstanz, 1949.

Reed, T. J. ' "Geist und Kunst." Thomas Mann's Abandoned Essay on Literature.' In *Oxford German Studies*, 1 (1966).

Scherrer, Paul, and Wysling, Hans. *Quellenkritische Studien zum Werk Thomas Manns*. Berne, 1967. The first volume of 'Thomas-Mann-Studien'.

Schröter, Klaus. *Thomas Mann*. Hamburg, 1964.

Stern, J. P. *Thomas Mann*. Columbia University Press, 1967.

Thomas, R. Hinton. *Thomas Mann: the Mediation of Art*. Oxford University Press, 1956.

(3) OTHER MATERIAL

Adorno, T. W. *Philosophie der neuen Musik*. Tübingen and Frankfurt, 1949. Second edition, 1958.

Butler, E. M. *The Fortunes of Faust*. Cambridge University Press, 1952.

Deussen, P. *Erinnerungen an Friedrich Nietzsche*. Leipzig, 1901.

Gray, R. D. *The German Tradition in Literature, 1871–1945*. Cambridge University Press, 1965.

Heller, Erich. *The Disinherited Mind*. Harmondsworth, Penguin, 1961. Latest hardback (third) edition, Bowes and Bowes, 1971.

HAJ Heller, Erich. *The Artist's Journey into the Interior and Other Essays*. Secker and Warburg, 1966.

JSM Jung, C. G. *The Spirit in Man, Art, and Literature*. Translated by R. F. C. Hull. Collected Works, Volume 15. Routledge and Kegan Paul, 1966.

NK *The Portable Nietzsche*. Writings of Nietzsche, edited and translated by Walter Kaufmann. New York, 1954. English hardback edition (same pagination), Chatto and Windus, 1971.

Reich, Willi. *Schoenberg*. Translated by Leo Black. Longman, 1971.

Rufer, Josef. *The Works of Arnold Schoenberg*. Translated by Dika Newlin. Faber and Faber, 1962.

Schoenberg, Arnold. *Letters*. Edited by Erwin Stein and translated by Eithne Wilkins and Ernst Kaiser. Faber and Faber, 1963.

Schoenberg, Arnold. *Style and Idea*. Edited and translated by Dika Newlin. Williams and Norgate, 1951.

Schoenberg, Arnold. 'Further to the Schoenberg-Mann Controversy.' Translated and annotated by Hans Keller. In *Music Survey*, 1949, Volume 2, Number 2.

Stuckenschmidt, H. H. *Arnold Schoenberg*. Translated by Edith Temple Roberts and Humphrey Searle. John Calder, 1959.

Index

This is principally an index of names, but it includes a list of all works by Mann which are referred to or quoted from in the text. It does not include names mentioned only in the Bibliography.